Growing Our Unity

19 Vital Practices for a Thriving Relationship

Susanne M. Alexander and W. Grant Peirce IV

Growing Our Unity

Trade Paperback ISBN: 978-1-940062-38-9
Trade eBook ISBN: 978-1-940062-39-6
Marriage Transformation PDF ISBN: 978-1-940062-40-2
Library of Congress Control Number: 2025938832

Publisher: Marriage Transformation LLC, USA
Printer: IngramSpark®, 14 Ingram Blvd, La Vergne, TN, USA

Contact Information: marriagetransformation.com
susanne@marriagetransformation.com; +1.423.599.0153

Growing Our Unity contains stories collected from individuals and couples, edited and shared anonymously. This book offers valuable and informative insights into couple relationships. If expert assistance is needed, please consult with a qualified professional counselor.

Cover Design and Model Graphic: Steiner Graphics

Layout: Marriage Transformation, LLC (There is no international punctuation placement and spelling standard, so the book contains a mix of British and American formats.)

Note: This book has been renamed and revised from the original work titled "Couple Vitality" by the same authors, published in 2022 by CharacterYAQ. Some of the testimonials included are for "Couple Vitality".

Appreciation for *Growing Our Unity*

From Couples and Individuals

"This is a fantastic guide to a healthy relationship. It will undoubtedly help many couples. Congratulations, and get it out into the world!" Glenn and Elisabeth

"This book is a great tool for really identifying what it takes to sustain a relationship. It's written in a manner that allows for deep self-reflection, and it clearly outlines the steps that are needed to achieve a vital relationship. The goals are realistic, transparent, and thoroughly explained, making it easy to recognize the strengths and areas that need to be addressed to optimize and improve a relationship." D. F.

"I like the use of Respect, Trust, Unity, and the other virtues as guides to reflection for the couples. A gift to the community and the world." Johanna Merritt Wu

"*Growing Our Unity* is an information-packed toolkit with a wealth of ideas and techniques that a couple can use as they need to deepen their relationship. With a wide range of topics, including discovering shared values, establishing a friendship, communicating about money, and many more, a couple can focus on areas they need to strengthen, or they can go through the book more systematically. I found the suggested exercises to be clear, helpful, and thought-provoking. I plan to return to this book many times as a valuable resource for communication about important topics and to improve my relationship." Anne Bivans

From Amazon.com:

- "5 out of 5 stars. Great resource to strengthen relationships. Great collection of insight and activities to improve communication and help understand and support a spouse better. Draws from many well-respected resources."
- "5 out of 5 stars. Great handbook. I found it very helpful. Did it save my marriage? Possibly! Things are good!"

From the US Review of Books (Kate Robinson)

"This engaging self-help volume rises to the task of systematically outlining how to develop and maintain a happy, fulfilling marriage. Authors Alexander and Peirce combine their decades of transformative life experience and career expertise in psychology to deftly describe the concrete, methodical steps couples can take to turn nearly broken relationships into friendly, accommodating unions that survive and thrive. The authors' enthusiasm for their topic shines through the six sections of well-organized themed chapters containing concrete steps and suggestions for 'Powerfully Creating Couple Unity,' 'Creating Shared Values and Vision,' 'Creating a Loving Partnership,' 'Creating Connecting Experiences,' 'Forging Deeper Connection,' and 'Expanding Beyond Us.'

"As described in the introduction, the accessible science-based tools and suggestions are designed to be actively practiced by couples as they navigate the highs and lows of their relationship. The foundation of the authors' system consists of 'Core Elements,' 'Unifiers,' and 'Virtues.' The concepts are embraceable as action steps to better understand partners' mutual and individual needs and responses. The system's flexibility allows couples to devise their own 'toolkits' of concepts to apply to their discussions, designed to reinforce clear communication and foster commitment and unity for individual and marital growth.

"Section One sets the stage with three foundational principles to study and practice before learning the nineteen 'Unifiers' described in succeeding chapters. The authors suggest that the first two sections are primarily foundational, and the remaining sections build upon these. Readers are encouraged to progress at their own pace, and the system is adaptable to the needs and preferences of different couples. ... Overall, the authors' helpful and practical book ticks all the boxes."

RECOMMENDED by the US Review
https://www.theusreview.com/reviews-1/Growing-Our-Unity-by-Susanne-M-Alexander-and-W-Grant-Peirce-IV.html

From Professional Colleagues

"This book is thorough, incredibly positive, and full of examples and strategies—exactly what couples need. I especially like the idea of a relationship as one of the best places to work on character and the book's clear theme of building character virtues. (I am reminded of one of my favorite Frank Pittman lines, 'marriage is your last best chance to grow up!'.) I applaud you for what is obviously a deep dive into the research to provide such a practical, positive guide for couples to truly create a thriving relationship. I am confident this information will help oh so many people." Pat Love, EdD, author of *The Truth About Love*

"This is an excellent resource for couples looking to strengthen their relationship and deepen their connection. It clearly and effectively explains important concepts needed to build a lasting love and offers practical exercises and tools the couple can use to explore themselves and their partners in a deeper, more meaningful way." David Grammer, Licensed Marriage and Family Therapist; Grammerfamilytherapy.com

"This book is the answer to many couples' prayers. Some are clearly in the dark, looking for a way out of the madness called their marriage or their relationship. They desperately want *Growing Our Unity*. This book gives them exactly that and so much more. If you want a better relationship and want to put your heart into making that happen, start reading tonight. Dreams do come true." Nisa Muhammad, DMin; weddedblissinc.com; founder of Black Marriage Day

"This book isn't for couples who want quick-fix tips or who are recreational dabblers into having a good relationship. It's for couples who are all in and understand how their relationship is the foundation for changing the world—for couples who want nothing less than complete transformation. Kudos to the authors for their in-depth yet approachable concepts." Priscilla Hunt, Executive Director, Better Marriages; bettermarriages.org; closecompanions.org

"I like the content of the book. I find the tie-in to virtues intriguing, and I like that it is character-based and not faith-based." Paul Kuhn, serving couples with his wife through their church and Better Marriages for 25+ years

Growing Our Unity Table of Contents

Welcome!

Creating a couple relationship can be one of the most wonderful and challenging experiences you undertake in your lives. It has highs, lows, joys, and moments when you're stuck in problems. Maintaining a relationship is a dynamic process of growth, so investing in it with consistent effort and persevering over time bring the most significant rewards. You can do it, and we are here to guide you.

You may be early in a relationship and want to establish a strong foundation with good habits that prevent problems. Or, you may be considering getting married and forming a family. Maybe you have been married for a long time and want to enhance your relationship. Alternatively, you may feel disconnected or hurt and struggle in your partnership. Whatever the state of your relationship, it's not too late to invest the time in learning new words, actions, and approaches that grow unity.

As professionals in virtues and relationships, we bring together for you some of the most important insights from science, stories from couples, personal experiences, and our own professional observations. We integrate the most powerful and dynamic aspect of your interactions that connect you as a couple: your character virtues. We will share with you how to use virtues as a new "language" of connection between you.

What Is a Thriving Relationship?

You create a thriving relationship by consistently applying this book's Core Elements and Unifiers. "Thriving" means that your couple relationship is alive, growing, and energizing for both of you. You appreciate being together, and the flow of energy between you is strong and positive. You can accomplish

1

many aspects of life together that would be more difficult as individuals. A powerful unity and connection are growing between you, and your sense of belonging increases:

> "… [I]t is only in the context of connection with others that our deepest needs can be met. Whether we like it or not, each of us has an unshakable dependence on others. … We need camaraderie, affection, love. These are not options in life, or sentimental trimmings; they are part of our species' survival kit. We *need* to belong."[1] Les and Leslie Parrott

Healthy couples make and keep a commitment to be together. Couple unity grows when two healthy individuals strive to be excellent partners to one another. They consciously act in relationship-enhancing ways from the beginning of their connection. They also choose to apply virtues to move their words and actions in a positive direction toward each other. They strive each day for new levels of growth and connection.

Growing, Virtues, and Becoming "Us"

This guide is packed with science-based tools and information to help you cultivate unity and enhance the quality of your relationship. As a couple, you will access the power to live, grow, and thrive. The earlier you learn and apply virtues-based habits, behavior patterns, and ways of interacting, the happier and more vibrant your relationship will be.

Every couple is unique, and you will develop your view of what couple unity looks and feels like for you. Below is one person's view.

"[Couples] ...have an intimate connection. They make joint decisions about life, talk about things before decisions are made, communicate love and respect to each other on a daily basis, and are able to talk about anything without fear of judgment, put-downs, or criticism. They have an intimate emotional connection. They could be away from each other for weeks due to work and come back and pick up a conversation right where they left off. They have a healthy and satisfying sex life. Their time together is as comfortable as their feet in a favorite pair of slippers on a cold winter night. They curl up in each other's arms, knowing they are loved, cared for, respected, appreciated, and listened to. Words don't even need to be exchanged all the time, because both husband and wife understand each other."[2] Kevin Leman

Does this describe a healthy couple relationship to you? Or would you want to create something different?

Here are some of the key concepts in this guide to accompany you:

- Two individuals come together and commit to creating a unified and interdependent partnership, which is a third entity, more than the sum of the two individuals. It includes their stories, histories, experiences, and creative outcomes, such as children and family, all of which are intertwined and cannot be separated.

- The two individuals become unified partners, integrating their individual needs into their partnership. They use words like "we", "us", and "ours" instead of "I", "me", and "mine".

- Each partner has virtue strengths and growth areas that dynamically affect the quality of a couple's interactions.

- As a couple reflects, consults, and interacts in virtue-based ways, they grow their unity and develop shared values and a vision for their relationship.

- Through developing and integrating virtues with specific actions, a couple creates unity in their relationship.

- They both strengthen their practice of the virtue of Unity, which empowers them to contribute to one another, the quality and unity of their relationship, and to others.

- A couple continually reflects, consults, interacts, builds connection, and increases commitment, which creates a thriving relationship.

- As they encourage each other and grow as a couple, they use the virtue of Creativity to celebrate together. The partners develop their virtues throughout their relationship-building process and increase their connection and well-being.

Note: There are 22 virtues focused on in *Growing Our Unity*. These 22 are listed below and described in "Core Element C: Virtues Growth". You might have noticed that "Creativity" and "Unity" were capitalized above. Throughout the book, when the 22 Virtues appear, they are Capitalized to draw your attention to them and to differentiate them from other uses of the words. The word is uncapitalized when the book content focuses on the state of unity.

1. Adherence
2. Compassion
3. Creativity
4. Dependability
5. Excellence
6. Flexibility
7. Honor
8. Humility
9. Justice
10. Moderation
11. Orderliness
12. Perseverance
13. Politeness and Sociability
14. Positive Spirit
15. Purposefulness
16. Reflection
17. Respect
18. Self-Discipline
19. Service
20. Trust
21. Truthfulness
22. Unity

These virtues are derived from the Character Foundations Assessment™, a validated instrument that author W. Grant Peirce IV developed. Taking this assessment may assist you in understanding your orientation toward each virtue and, subsequently, in implementing the content of this book. You can contact either of the authors to take the assessment individually and receive an accompanying insights session with either of them or with another certified practitioner. See "About the Authors and Our Contact Information" at the end of the book.

Customize Your Approach

It's best if you take the content of this guide, pay close attention to the principles and their application, and then customize your approach to create a couple relationship full of unity that works for the two of you. Some suggestions are provided in the next section. You may also seek additional sources of information or consider consulting a professional.

5

In this guide, we illuminate the path to healthy relationships and highlight the importance of incorporating virtue-based words and actions at every stage of your journey. We have seen the benefit with our own marriage partners and also in our clients' relationships, and we are confident that this is the way to a better future for you.

Welcome to *Growing Our Unity*!

Susanne M. Alexander and W. Grant Peirce IV

Suggestions for How to Use This Guide

Determining Your Approach

Using this guide will be interesting, fun, and challenging. It will empower you to assemble a practical toolkit with information, ideas, and techniques you can utilize as needed. This guide is like a blueprint, and you're the builders of your relationship. It's likely wise to start with one easier goal and gradually add in more as you gain strengths.

Near the end of this guide, there's a section called "Reflecting and Consulting on Our Vital Practices". As you go through the content and activities, note any actions you want to continue to maintain the quality of your relationship. You may find it useful to look ahead to that section now.

Each chapter and Unifier includes a key concept, and you will determine together how much time to spend on each one. You may already be skilled at the focus of a particular chapter and choose to spend your time on others. Your lives are probably full of many activities, so making regular dates with each other to discuss this material and carry out activities will keep it a high priority.

You may discover it's challenging to study together or that you have limited time available. If so, you may delegate or take turns, with one of you doing the study and sharing key points with the other. Then, discuss the section together. If one of you is unlikely to read the book, the other might read it and apply the learning, which in turn will help the other see their positive example and appreciate practicing it themselves.

Your efforts to grow your unity may feel intense at times. As needed, please take a break for relaxation, social time, and conversation, which also increase your unity and well-being.

Overview of the Sections

Section 1: Powerfully Creating Couple Unity

The book begins with chapters that introduce you to three Core Elements in "Section 1: Powerfully Creating Couple Unity". These are listed below.

1. Unity
2. Reflection and Consultation
3. Virtues Growth

These are foundational elements for your relationship, so it's essential that you read about them before studying the 19 Unifiers. Unity is the ultimate goal of any relationship. You will continuously use "Reflection and Consultation" and "Virtues Growth" as you energize and grow your relationship.

These elements are *big* concepts, so Section 1 is only a brief introduction. You will grow to understand them more over time as you practice the actions throughout the guide.

Section 2: Creating Shared Values and Vision

Next, please proceed to "Section 2: Creating Shared Values and Vision". Here, you will begin to utilize the first three Unifiers to prioritize your relationship, clarify the values that are important to you both, and discern your shared vision for the relationship. You will examine the concept of commitment and how it assists you to apply Perseverance in creating a relationship filled with unity.

- Unifier 1: Prioritizing Our Relationship
- Unifier 2: What Is Important to Us?
- Unifier 3: Where Are We Going?

Sections 3-6:

After completing the first two sections, you will have established a great foundation. Then, you can decide how you want to proceed with the Unifiers in Sections 3-6. There are many possibilities:

a. You can study and implement the Unifiers in numerical order.
b. You can focus on the topics where you most need unity.
c. You can begin with a topic you already think you're quite good at, so you're encouraged to keep going.
d. You can quickly read through all the content and then focus on specific areas to spend more time on.
e. You can spend a few months going slowly through each Unifier, and then revisit the topics for review once a year.
f. You can group topics as a "quest": an initiative and focus that you think will benefit your relationship the most. For example, if your quest is to cherish one another, you might choose Unifier 7, which focuses on love, Unifier 8, which emphasizes appreciation, and Unifier 13, which highlights giving thoughtful service.
g. Your own creative approach.

Section 3: Creating a Loving Partnership

- Unifier 4: Establishing Our Friendship
- Unifier 5: Understanding Each Other
- Unifier 6: Respecting Each Other
- Unifier 7: Loving One Another
- Unifier 8: Appreciating One Another
- Unifier 9: Harmonizing Our Communications

Section 4: Creating Connecting Experiences

- Unifier 10: Choosing to Merge
- Unifier 11: Enjoying Social Time
- Unifier 12: Sharing Laughter and Humor
- Unifier 13: Giving Thoughtful Service

Section 5: Forging Deeper Connection

- Unifier 14: Communicating About Sex
- Unifier 15: Managing Our Money
- Unifier 16: Growing from Difficulties
- Unifier 17: Resolving and Rebounding

Section 6: Expanding Beyond Us

- Unifier 18: Establishing Family Harmony
- Unifier 19: Connecting with Friends and Community

You have your unique couple relationship, and you will creatively apply this guide uniquely toward having a healthy, happy, and unified connection. It will be good to apply Flexibility to determine the best approach for your journey as a couple.

The Focus on Virtues

Every book about relationships is unique, varying in topic and author expertise. In this case, we are specialists on the topic of virtues, so you will read introductory material about that and then see the emphasis on the virtues throughout. [See "Core Element C: Virtues Growth".]

We believe that couples can commit to each other and choose to raise the quality of their partnership. If you aim to create unity and maintain a thriving relationship over time, this guide will be your companion, a book you refer to often. *Growing Our Unity* provides actions you can take to make improvements quickly. However, the content is also designed to be a significant and ongoing part of your life.

Enriching Your Experience

You will gain new perspectives as you increasingly incorporate the concepts in *Growing in Unity* into your life. Including elements of the arts in your life can enhance your learning and the quality of your relationship. Your activities may include music, drawing, dance, poetry, journal-writing, photography, or other uses of Creativity to enhance your learning and understanding. Incorporating the arts generates joy and draws you closer together.

From Your Viewpoint As a Couple

You will notice that most of the book is written in the voice of a couple who is deeply engaged in the process of growing their couple unity. The pronouns used are ones like "we" and "our". These pronouns invite you to identify with the content, see yourselves as partners, and engage in the discussed behaviors. "We" isn't the authors, who are colleagues and not a couple.

About Timing

Growing Our Unity can be useful for couples at any relationship stage when they want to strengthen, grow, or heal their relationship and adopt new behaviors individually and as a couple. *It's a learning tool for preventing issues.* Couples may also find it beneficial to work with a mentor-couple, coach, or counselor, along with learning.

This guide is *not as suitable for individuals and couples in the middle of a significant crisis*, such as excessively using drugs or alcohol, being in an unsafe situation, or experiencing violence or trauma. These couples will benefit from professional help and healing before attempting to strengthen their relationships, at which point this guide may be useful.

Growing Our Unity—A Dynamic Process
Overview of the Model

Achieving couple unity is an ongoing, dynamic process that strengthens the core aspects of a relationship. The model below illustrates this process, highlighting **3 Core Elements** and **5 Dimensions of Couple Unity**. The **19 Unifiers** explored in this book are distributed across these 5 dimensions, providing actionable steps for deepening connection and harmony.

The 3 Core Elements

The model includes 3 foundational elements that support every Couple Unifier:

1. **Unity** – The ultimate goal of any relationship, symbolizing a deep and lasting bond between partners. Its place is at the center of the model.

2. **Reflection & Consultation** – Continuous practices that help couples understand themselves and one another, grow through open and respectful dialogue, navigate challenges, and make and carry out decisions.

3. **Virtues Growth** – The development of positive character virtues such as Respect, Dependability, and Humility. These positively influence the partners' words and behaviors, build unity in their relationship, and enhance mutual understanding.

Reflection & Consultation and **Virtues Growth** are depicted as parallel circles surrounding Unity, emphasizing their ongoing role in the unifying process.

The 5 Dimensions of Couple Unity

These 5 dimensions represent the key areas where couples actively build their relationship:

1. **Creating Shared Values and Vision** – Establishing a common purpose and guiding principles.

2. **Creating a Loving Partnership** – Fostering mutual care, support, and teamwork.

3. **Creating Connecting Experiences** – Increasing closeness through shared activities and meaningful moments.

4. **Forging Deeper Connection** – Strengthening emotional, intellectual, and physical intimacy.

5. **Expanding Beyond Us** – Extending love and unity to family, friends, and the broader community.

These dimensions are interconnected and continuously evolving, empowering couples to nurture their relationship while also fostering unity beyond themselves. As couples engage in this process, they progressively achieve **the ultimate goal: lasting unity**.
The model is shown below.

Growing Our Unity
A Dynamic Process

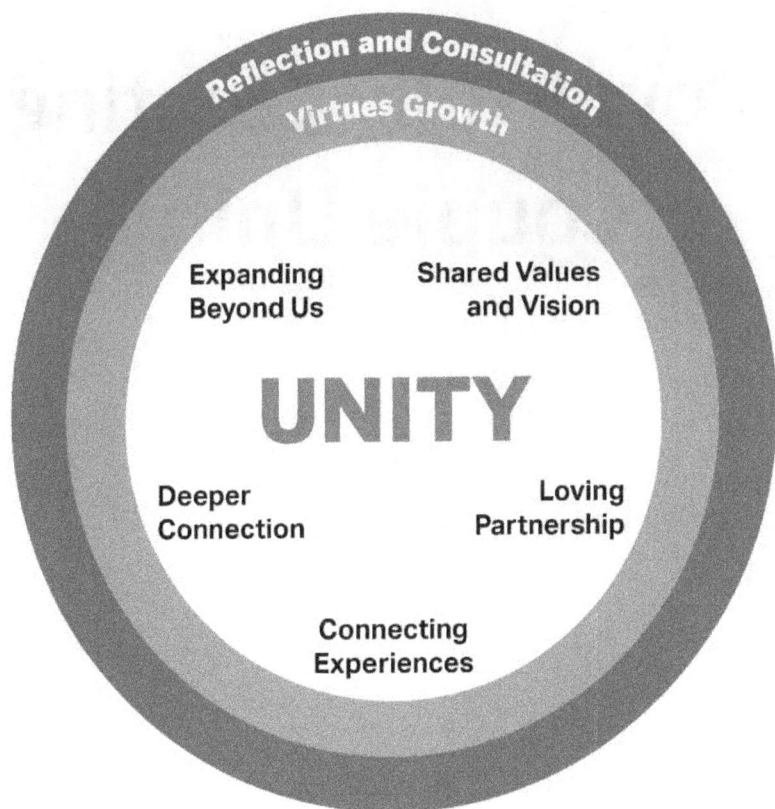

Reflection and Consultation

Virtues Growth

Expanding
Beyond Us

Shared Values
and Vision

UNITY

Deeper
Connection

Loving
Partnership

Connecting
Experiences

Section 1:

Powerfully Creating Couple Unity

Section 1 Introduction

Relationships thrive and couples grow in unity when you consistently apply three essential elements. This section introduces you to these elements you will practice throughout the guide as you focus on the 19 Unifiers. In this first section, you will learn about the importance of:

- **Core Element A: Commitment to Unity**—Unity is the "glue" that holds you together and enables you to function in harmony. It includes being fair with each other and maintaining your connection as a couple. While you may not always agree, when unity is a shared goal, it provides a strong impetus for navigating disagreements effectively. You consider the impact of your words and actions and their potential to create unity or cause disunity, and you choose to communicate and act in ways that grow your unity instead.

- **Core Element B: Reflection and Consultation**—It contributes to your unity when you reflect on your words and actions as individuals and assess their effectiveness. Unity also grows when you're skillful as a couple in reflecting and consulting to build understanding and reach unified decisions. These two skills apply to every aspect of your life together.

- **Core Element C: Virtues Growth**—Sometimes, you may think about your unique personalities and how they affect your relationship and interactions. However, you will discover in this guide that your virtues are even more vital to focus on, partly because you have significant power to grow and develop them. When you each have many virtue strengths and apply them for the good of each

16

other and your relationship, you will avoid the conflicts that often arise when virtues require significant growth.

The topics here in Section 1 are themes throughout the book. You will have opportunities to build your skills with them in each Unifier.

Core Element A: Commitment to Unity

"... [W]ith unity in diversity, we grow together through a true realization of our wider potential and primal oneness."
Raymond and Furugh Switzer

Focus Statement: We strive to create a state of harmony, connection, and oneness of our minds, hearts, and souls, which leads to harmonizing our thoughts, feelings, words, and actions.

Deeper Learning:

All the Parts Contribute

We love the concept of "unity", and we see it as a powerful state for us to strive for in our relationship. However, we realize that the concept is complex, as is our journey to complete unity.

To achieve a state of unity as a couple, both of us individually practice the virtue of Unity. As we include later in "Core Element C: Virtues Growth", this virtue is described as follows:

"With Unity, we:

- Build harmony and consensus through effective communication and consultation.
- Collaborate to develop common vision, purpose, and goals with individuals, groups, and communities.
- Align personal goals and activities with those of the group.
- Embrace the diversity of people and welcome them into a full range of activities.

- Strive to create a sense of belonging and oneness between people."

We also recognize that the virtue of Reflection and the couple communication practice of consultation are vital contributors to creating our state of unity. These are discussed in the next chapter, "Core Element B: Reflection and Consultation". Our ability to reflect on our actions, individually and collectively, keeps us honest. Bringing all topics to the forefront and consulting about them helps build understanding and enables us to make effective decisions, keeping us in tune and moving in unity together.

The Unifiers, which are covered in most of the other chapters of this book, refine our words and actions to enable us to live more consistently in a state of unity. We contribute to this unity through a shared vision, turning toward one another, laughing, socializing, and more.

[**Note:** For clarity, the virtue of Unity is one of the 22 virtues focused on in the book, and these are Capitalized throughout the book. When the content focuses on the state of unity, the word is uncapitalized.]

Unity and Well-Being

We began our relationship as two individuals with separate lives. Our couple journey is about how we come together, what we love and appreciate in each other, and what becomes our shared identity. We, in essence, create something new: our partnership. Throughout this process, we still retain our individual personalities, characters, and behaviors. We influence these aspects as we interact and connect, keeping our partnership energized and harmonious.

As we cultivate a healthy relationship, unity is at its core. This may not yet be a common term in our relationship, but increasing our focus on cultivating it will yield many positive outcomes between us. Creating unity invites us to view our relationship as being a single unit that cannot be divided. If we associate oneness with our relationship, it shifts our viewpoint and actions in a new way.

When we are united, we:

- Place the health and strength of our relationship above self-interest
- Focus on points of commonality and agreement
- Collaborate on all actions and decisions that affect our relationship or family
- Operate with fairness, Respect, and equality
- Feel a deep connection of love between us

We Are Still Individuals

Of course, since we still retain our personalities and who we are as people, being united isn't about losing ourselves in being a couple. It's also not about agreeing all the time or having everything in common, as different viewpoints can spark new ways of looking at a situation. It's not about dominating each other into an unwilling agreement either. It's about valuing our harmony so that we are motivated to function as a team and be our best selves. We connect in healthy ways with each other:

"A healthy marriage is the union of two individuated, differentiated persons. These are people truly capable of loving the uniqueness of each other. Thus, the union of marriage is not ever intended to be enmeshment or unity in conformity, as this would attenuate who we can truly be.

Rather, with unity in diversity, we grow together through a true realization of our wider potential and primal oneness. Mindful differentiation always develops through connection, not disconnection."[3] Raymond and Furugh Switzer

Our commitment to unity raises our awareness of when our interactions cause unwanted disunity and disconnection. As we increase our appreciation for unity and decrease our tolerance for disunity, we become more drawn to each other and strive to deepen our connection. With focus, effort, and practice, we discover new ways to create unity every day.

Striving for "We" and "Us"

We begin interactions consciously focused on unity, creating more unity through the quality of our words and actions, and strive to achieve unified outcomes. We practice Dependability in carrying out positive actions and pursuing goals that keep us connected for the long term. Unity keeps our relationship growing.

As we strengthen our unity, carrying out the actions that connect us becomes easier. We aren't upset or anxious with each other, and our happiness with each other increases our ability to contribute to our home, work, and community. Our commitment to keeping our unity strong shows in these ways:

"Research has shown that couples who maintain and act on dedication are more connected, happier, and more open with each other. That's because dedicated partners show their commitment in the following very specific ways...:

- They think more like a team, with a strong orientation toward 'us' and 'we'.
- They make their partner and marriage a high priority.
- They protect their relationship from attraction to others.
- They sacrifice for one another without resentment.
- They invest of themselves in building a future together—they have a long-term view."[4]

Scott M. Stanley

When we behave like teammates on the same side, we experience a sense of unity. As we ensure we protect our relationship, contribute to it, and envision staying together, our unity becomes a powerful source of good for us and others.

Science demonstrates the vital necessity of "close connections to other people, and deep connections to moral and spiritual meaning". We are "hardwired to connect". Here's why: "Meeting these basic needs for connection is essential to health and to human flourishing."[5] "Hardwired to Connect"

When we have a secure connection with someone we care about, we are:

- Better at seeking and giving support
- More curious and more open to new information
- More flexible and open to new experiences
- More confident about solving problems
- More likely to successfully achieve goals[6]

Summarized from Dr. Sue Johnson

To have unity, we must be strong in the virtues of Truthfulness, Justice, Respect, and Trust. When we apply these virtues to our choices, responsibilities, and communications, our relationship improves and is protected from harm.

Unity keeps us aware of our relationship's greater context and importance rather than being inward-centered. Our union has a positive influence on our extended family, the social structure of our community, and even society as a whole. How amazing this is! As a result, we feel even more motivated to strive for unity as a couple and a family.

In the following two chapters, we will explore new ways to grow our unity. In "Core Element B: Reflection and Consultation," we will explore how reflecting and communicating with one another enhances our understanding and fosters a closer connection. In "Core Element C: Virtues Growth", we will learn how to effectively grow and practice the virtues necessary for creating unity and sustaining our relationship.

Examples:

- Planning a special event to acknowledge a beloved family member or friend
- Waiting to address a problem until our partner can be fully involved
- Speaking positively about our partner to people
- Practicing Trust for us each to handle agreed-upon tasks
- Stopping actions that are upsetting to our partner
- Celebrating anniversaries of special milestones

Applying Virtues:

Below are some practical ways to incorporate virtues into daily practices with the theme of this chapter.

Purposefulness
- Encourage each other to grow and achieve our shared dreams.

- Collaborate and agree on action steps to fulfill goals, and carry them out.
- Support our long-term health by planning and cooking nutritious meals and organizing consistent exercise.

Respect
- Listen carefully, paying attention to what is important in each other's lives and offering solutions when invited.
- Speak to each other as adult partners, not in the voice or role of a parent or child.
- Observe, recognize, and utilize our strengths and abilities.

Unity
- Share thoughts, feelings, and laughter about what is happening in our lives.
- Turn toward our partner to address issues as a team.
- Focus on our positive qualities and actions and those of our family members.

Learning Activities:

1. Identify a couple that we think is quite unified. Observe their words and actions, and consult with them about how they maintain unity and prevent or resolve disunity.

2. Collaborate with planning and carrying out a special occasion in our relationship or family.

Couple Reflection and Consultation:

Throughout this couple guide, there are invitations to practice the virtue of Reflection about your interactions and connection. This practice gives you opportunities to celebrate progress and consult to address issues.

1. What would demonstrate that we are unified in our functioning?
2. In what ways does feeling unified affect our well-being and relationship?
3. In what ways does feeling disunified affect our well-being and relationship?
4. What actions can we take to grow our unity when our relationship appears to be out of harmony?
5. How could increasing kindness or thoughtfulness between us influence our level of unity?
6. How can we utilize laughter and humor to grow our unity?
7. What new ideas for growing unity and increasing our connection are now coming to mind? How will we carry them out?

Core Element B: Reflection and Consultation

"... [N]ine times out of ten, conflicts may be resolved
when couples step into each other's shoes."
Les and Leslie Parrott and David H. Olson

Focus Statement: We reflect as individuals, and we use consultation to reflect together, both of which deepen our understanding of each other and various issues and empower us to make effective decisions as needed.

Deeper Learning:

Creating couple unity has many facets, and it will take time for us to work collaboratively on increasing it. Learning new ways to develop an excellent relationship is exciting, and we will enjoy celebrating our progress and growing closer.

Two linked communication practices will support our growth process. The first is applying the virtue of Reflection, which we use to gain insights as individuals and as a couple. The second practice is consultation, which we use to build understanding and reach agreement on matters. Doing both Reflection and consultation well will take Perseverance and Excellence, so we will be patient and kind with each other as we learn.

Reflection

Reflection allows us to pause, breathe, and gain new perspectives. We use Reflection when we need to consider what we have done, why, and the outcome, which often requires us to practice Humility. Reflection builds our understanding of ourselves and one another. We can use it to learn about what did and did not work well.

26

We often use Reflection as individuals, but it can also be done together. Below are some of its elements. We:

- Calmly build self-awareness and understanding as we assess ourselves
- Explore to understand our actions, thoughts, feelings, and perceptions about a situation
- Analyze to gain insights into potential approaches and actions for improving behaviors and circumstances
- Seek inspiration and new insights to address issues and ways to keep creating unity in our relationship
- Visualize ourselves as a unified entity

When an interaction between us becomes intense and potentially disunifying, we can stop speaking, take time to calm down, and use Reflection individually. Then, we can come back together more peacefully, calmly share our insights, and create outcomes in unity.

As we improve our ability to engage in Reflection, we better understand our motives, goals, personal history, and reasons for reactions. We share our new perspectives and gain further ones as we interact. We also increase our ability to adjust or to change our viewpoints and approaches completely.

Consultation

"Consultation" is a word that can have multiple meanings, so we will learn how it applies to couples as part of the process of creating couple unity. It's a type of dialogue designed to build understanding between us and to assist us in effectively achieving unified decisions. We can use it to explore our thoughts, feelings, wishes, needs, expectations, and other aspects of ourselves. We can determine our actions to take and what each of us will do to fulfill our decisions. As with any skill, learning takes time, and we will have opportunities to practice it frequently.

When done well, consultation can significantly enhance our harmony and reduce the frequency of conflict between us. A communication practice like this is particularly useful for us as a couple, as there's no majority vote to settle different viewpoints, unlike in a group consultation.

Consulting together requires us to apply Truthfulness and Trust with each other. These virtues assist us in being vulnerable and sharing what is on our hearts and minds. Truthful words can sometimes cause pain in our hearts, so pairing them with other virtues is essential. Applying Compassion and keeping our words kind can make it easier for us to stay mentally and emotionally present, listen carefully, and build our understanding. Here is some wisdom:

> "... [R]esearch shows that as much as 90 percent of marital spats can be resolved if all the couple does is accurately see the issue from each other's perspective. Don't miss this point: nine times out of ten, conflicts may be resolved when couples step into each other's shoes."[7]
> Les and Leslie Parrott and David H. Olson

Consultations may be informal or formal, unstructured or structured, and quick or time-consuming. When we apply Flexibility, we choose the approach that fits us and the issue we are consulting about. Consultation can have formal elements, such as an agenda or advance fact-finding, especially when a significant decision is to be made. However, as we integrate consultation into all aspects of our relationship, we discover how to flow with the process more informally.

We often consult while doing activities as a couple, such as eating, walking, traveling, or cuddling in a comfortable sitting area. We may start consulting on a topic and then set it aside to allow time for Reflection. Often, a quick consultation takes two text exchanges on our phones, and it's done. At other times, we may revisit a topic in person for weeks before it's clear we are in harmony about a decision.

Consultation is a process that invites us to generate inspirational ideas throughout. Before consulting, we use silent Reflection or prayer to welcome these ideas. Sometimes, we invite experts to consult with us, such as for financial planning, or we ask family members to participate if a topic involves them. We decide ahead of time if we will get their input and then make a private decision, or whether they will be fully involved in making a group decision with us all together.

Key Aspects of Couple Consultation:

1. We collaborate as partners to build understanding about what is true for us and/or to make unified decisions.

2. We strive to have pure motives and demonstrate a Positive Spirit of goodwill about each other's intentions.

3. We are willing to listen with Humility and learn, stay calm and composed, and apply Perseverance through difficulties.

4. We clarify and agree on the topic we are addressing and determine whether we have the facts needed to proceed.

5. We seek to understand each other through careful listening, summarizing what we have said as needed.

6. We openly share our thoughts, feelings, and factual details.

7. We contribute equally to the process, which includes freely sharing information, offering opinions for consideration in a calm and composed way, and seeking to understand and gain new insights.

8. We are committed to discovering the truth, which can emerge in various ways, including from different—and even apparently clashing—viewpoints.

9. After we share something, it belongs to neither of us; this central pooling of contributions frees us to practice Flexibility and be open-minded to receive new information and use it for our common purpose; we merge ideas as appropriate, and we determine together the best outcome.

10. We avoid feeling hurt in the process of fully examining what is true for us, which we assist with a loving and kind atmosphere.

11. We stay focused centrally on what we are creating together, and we don't position ourselves on opposite sides; there's only one side: Our Side.

12. We reach a mutually agreeable conclusion about what we have newly understood or about a decision on what is best to do, often something new that neither of us thought of before.

13. We carry out decisions and plans in unity, so it becomes clear if we are not going in a positive direction; when some aspect isn't going smoothly, we can consult and change

direction rather than blame or criticize each other or our initial decision.

14. At times, we consult and cannot reach an agreement, and then we make a mutual decision for one of us to take the lead and begin action with the support of the other; we mutually encourage and assist each other while carrying out actions, so our unity is protected.

15. While implementing a decision, we check in and re-consult to assess the situation and determine if any changes are needed.

16. We happily express appreciation or celebrate when we complete carrying out a decision.

Consultation requires us to be collaborative, where we strive together to reach positive outcomes. Here is a description of speaking in this way:

"The tone of collaborative dialogue is friendly. Even when the topic is a serious one, the tone still feels cooperative, as if you have placed your problem on a table and the two of you have sat down side by side to try to solve it. You feel that you are confronting the problem together, rather than that you are confronting each other.

"Another tip-off that dialogue is collaborative is that you feel a sense of forward movement as you accumulate shared understanding. Adversarial dialogue feels repetitious. When dialogue is cooperative, with each successive comment you feel movement toward a shared plan of action."[8] Susan Heitler

We have observed that learning the skill of consulting as a couple is a gradual, experiential, and dynamic process that takes time. The more we incorporate it into our lives, the more natural it feels, and the more unity we grow. We stay aware of when we can consult quickly, but there will always be times when we must slow down the pace. This will give us enough time to utilize Reflection, gather sufficient facts, understand and express our thoughts and feelings, and fully address the issue.

We appreciate feeling unified, and we increasingly see how Reflection and consultation contribute to our unity. It's becoming clearer that virtues such as Respect and Self-Discipline are essential to achieve productive and unified consultations. "Virtues Growth" is the next Core Element in this section. In addition, the Unifiers covered in "Section 3: Creating a Loving Partnership" will contribute to the quality of our consultations.

Applying Virtues:

Below are some practical ways to incorporate virtues into daily practices with the theme of this chapter.

Purposefulness
- Turn to each other daily to consult about the issues that arise in our lives.
- Carry out tasks, activities, and projects, determining when we can do so together and when it's better to do them alone or with other people.
- Check in periodically to review progress toward achieving our goals and dreams.

Reflection

- Think about and then consult about our words and actions, noting what was beneficial and identifying what we want to improve.
- Consider the virtues we applied (or didn't) and those we strengthened each day.
- Determine a place where quiet thought can more easily occur, and spend time there each day.

Respect

- Talk with and listen to each other as equal partners.
- Show confidence in and appreciation for what each of us contributes.
- Address our well-being before, throughout, and after consultations, which could include rest, eating, or quiet reflection time.

Learning Activities:

1. Explore different methods of using Reflection to see what is most useful for each of us under various circumstances. Some ideas might include meditation, journal-writing, walking in nature, or gently asking each other exploratory and curious questions.

2. Share some positive memories from the early stages of our relationship. What feelings arise as we reflect on these previous experiences? Is there something we did then that we want to do again now?

3. Experiment with consulting in different locations, with or without another activity happening (examples: walking, driving, cooking...), and with and without physical closeness, eye contact, or touch. Reflect and consult about

what we felt was positive, what did not work well, and what we want to try again to strive for improvement.

4. Select a relatively minor topic that requires our attention. Pause to reflect on it separately and then together. Then, engage in consultation to create a solution acceptable to us. Try out the new solution and reflect on the outcome.

Couple Reflection and Consultation:

Throughout this couple guide, there are invitations to practice the virtue of Reflection about your interactions and connection. This practice gives you opportunities to celebrate progress and consult to address issues.

1. What works well for us to say and do before we start consulting? (examples: moment of quiet, prayer, glasses of water, snacks, ways to make notes...)
2. What topics are easy for us to manage? Which are more difficult?
3. When issues arise that we cannot easily resolve, how do we manage them?
4. Where could we benefit from increased skill-building and practice? (examples:
   a. Reducing defensive reactions when hearing an idea or opinion
   b. Being more open to each other's input during consultations and avoiding criticism
   c. Listening effectively and resisting the urge to interrupt
5. Applying Compassion and Respect)
6. When is it useful for us to use consultation to build understanding rather than to make a decision?
7. When has expecting a decision to be perfect stopped us from moving forward?

8. When is it essential to postpone action and keep striving for a better and more unified decision?

Core Element C: Virtues Growth

"The stability of our lives depends on our character."
Frank Pittman

Focus Statement: We apply and strengthen the virtues we have developed throughout our lives that guide our choices about thinking, speaking, and acting in beneficial ways.

Deeper Learning:

What Are Virtues?

We are born with the capacity to develop many positive virtues throughout our lives. We consider these virtues as essential parts of our characters. As we develop these virtues, they positively influence our thoughts, words, and actions. The resulting positive behaviors then improve our couple interactions and grow our unity.

Each of the 19 Unifiers in the following chapters will include ways to strengthen and appreciate our virtues. Their growth is a daily activity and ongoing process, so we do our best to be patient with ourselves and each other as we grow.

"The stability of our lives depends on our character. It is character, not passion, that keeps marriages together long enough to do their work of raising children into mature, responsible, productive citizens. In this imperfect world, it is character that enables people to survive, to endure, and to transcend their misfortunes."[9] Frank Pittman

We each have virtue strengths, and we appreciate different strengths in one another. Our feelings of love toward each other are often because we love each other's virtues.

When we discuss which are most important to us, we usually struggle to choose. However, Respect (described below) is one that we try to have as a consistent practice. Respect ensures that our consultations are positive and productive, which grows the unity in our relationship.

Virtue Descriptions

Below is a list of 22 virtues and a description of each. These virtues are drawn from the Character Foundations Assessment™, a validated instrument that author W. Grant Peirce IV developed. When these 22 virtues occur throughout this book, they are capitalized to draw attention to them.

You're probably familiar enough with the topics of character and virtues to notice that this list could include many more. While this list will guide you for now, you can add other virtues, such as patience, fidelity, or loyalty, to your daily actions over time.

Note: Taking the Character Foundations Assessment™ may assist you to understand your orientation toward each virtue and, subsequently, in implementing the content of this book. You can contact either of the authors to take the assessment and receive an accompanying insights session with either of them or with another certified practitioner. See "About the Authors and Our Contact Information" at the end of the book.

22 Virtues and Their Descriptions
1. **Adherence:** Align behavior with established rules, standards, and laws. Follow instructions and comply with agreements. Implement processes and tasks accurately and effectively. Observe safety and risk-reduction protocols that ensure the well-being and security of all involved.
2. **Compassion:** Listen deeply to and understand a person's feelings and circumstances. Care about a person's well-being. Provide emotional solace for a person's pain. Share comfort and alleviate suffering. Treat a person with mercy, giving them chances to try again for the potential benefit of all. Understand people's actions, offer forgiveness, and let go of negative reactions toward them, such as anger or judgment.
3. **Creativity:** Generate new ideas, products, and outcomes from accessing diverse resources. Think freely and look broadly for insights and connections, allowing for unique, innovative, and breakthrough solutions to emerge. Convert imaginative ideas into tangible artistic expressions.
4. **Dependability:** Make and keep promises and commitments. Prepare for timely and appropriate action. Act reliably and consistently. Accept accountability in words and actions. Choose wisely based on assessing priorities, capabilities, availability, and resources.
5. **Excellence:** Set and achieve high standards and deliver a superior quality of work. Go beyond acceptable standards and create beautiful and valuable outcomes. Learn and improve from experiences to develop expertise, skills, and mastery over time. Align efforts to contribute to positive, impactful results.

6. **Flexibility:** Respond to change, uncertainty, new experiences, and surprises with composure and grace. Adjust and adapt nimbly in response to varied people, perspectives, and situations. Accommodate different methods, ideas, and viewpoints. Accept and implement innovative approaches to evolving needs and circumstances.

7. **Honor:** Live up to high ethical and moral standards. Hold and consistently apply clear values and principles to words, actions, and decisions, and resist pressure or temptation to violate them. Actively encourage and support people to stay true to their values or principles, and recognize people for living up to them. Foster an environment of high ethical and moral standards.

8. **Humility:** Possess a balanced and realistic sense of self that includes awareness of strengths, limitations, accomplishments, and failures. Offer time, knowledge, and talents in a modest way. Strive to be open to feedback, learning, and self-improvement. Seek and accept people's knowledge, skills, and help. Turn toward people, listen to them, and encourage them to share their perspectives. Express appreciation for collective rather than individual accomplishments.

9. **Justice:** Initiate decisions, agreements, or actions based on clear facts that are free of bias and prejudice. Make proactive and objective observations of people's behaviors. Treat people fairly, considering all aspects of their situations, and protecting their rights as appropriate. Assign responsibilities in a balanced way and administer appropriate rewards, consequences, or corrective actions.

10. **Moderation:** Recognize and avoid extremes in use of time, energy, attention, words, and other choices. Achieve balanced well-being in relationships, work,

community service, exercise, and leisure activities. Monitor and manage the intensity of thoughts and emotions to achieve equilibrium and harmony. Consciously control excessive behaviors, impulses, and desires to achieve a sustainable lifestyle.

11. **Orderliness:** Live and work with a focused, organized, and calm mindset. Develop structured methods, processes, and systems. Maintain tidy, well-organized, clean, and welcoming spaces. Develop habits and efficient routines to find everything easily, manage time, create plans, and carry out tasks.

12. **Perseverance:** Apply patient and persistent effort and energy toward worthwhile goals. Overcome obstacles and bounce back from challenges, stay focused, and continue forward. Engage in consistent actions that lead to future rewards, even when there are no immediate benefits.

13. **Politeness and Sociability:** Demonstrate an approachable, outgoing, and positive social attitude in various settings. Show gracious and warm consideration for people, interacting with appropriate courtesy. Spend time having great conversations with people, mutually listening and sharing with each other. Build many types of lasting friendships and relationships.

14. **Positive Spirit:** Maintain a happy, hopeful, and uplifting attitude that inspires people. Celebrate the best in relationships, work, and service. Encourage people and lift their spirits with joy and laughter. Approach tasks and life with enthusiasm, energy, and vigor. Take a light-hearted approach to whatever arises. Maintain an optimistic view that challenges will be overcome and solutions will emerge.

15. **Purposefulness:** Pursue life aspirations, significant commitments, and long-term goals. Dedicate time and

energy toward achieving a vision or completing specific endeavors. Make decisive and courageous choices to participate in vital activities that contribute to meaningful and fulfilling outcomes.

16. **Reflection:** Analyze and learn from experiences and study best practices. Understand emotions and behaviors through self-awareness and assessing life circumstances. Take responsibility for actions and identify personal growth opportunities. Explore thoughts, ideas, and perceptions through inward musings. Seek answers to questions and look for inspiration for future actions.

17. **Respect:** Show esteem for people as fellow human beings. Listen to, understand, and appreciate people's diverse perspectives, feelings, and accomplishments. Value people's knowledge, skills, talents, and abilities. Interact with people with courtesy and fairness. Uphold the rights and opportunities of everyone.

18. **Self-Discipline:** Use inner control to set priorities and promptly perform important tasks. Regulate emotions and respond to people and situations in appropriate and positive ways. Engage in personal improvement and growth. Develop consistent and constructive habits. Focus on carrying out what is beneficial or productive and resist what is harmful or distracting.

19. **Service:** Consider thoughtfully the needs of people. Reach out with positive intent to be generous, helpful, and kind. Uplift people, foster their well-being, and work with them to achieve their goals. Act selflessly, consistently, and often sacrificially for people without expecting reward or recognition. Collaborate on efforts that benefit a person, group, or community.

20. **Trust:** Demonstrate confidence in people's good intentions, reliability, integrity, and ethical principles.

Show faith in people's ability to carry out new tasks. Embrace mistakes as opportunities for growth. Express gratitude for people's positive words, efforts, and actions. Build secure relationships that allow for open and honest sharing of private, confidential, or sensitive information.

21. **Truthfulness:** Recognize and accurately communicate facts and feelings. Behave with authenticity and honesty. Align values, words, and actions. Seek independent sources of information and integrate them to understand the reality of people, circumstances, and issues. Win the confidence of people through fact-based words, even when conveying them is difficult.

22. **Unity:** Build harmony and consensus through effective communication and consultation. Collaborate to develop common vision, purpose, and goals with individuals, groups, and communities. Align personal goals and activities with those of the group. Embrace the diversity of people and welcome them into a full range of activities. Strive to create a sense of belonging and oneness between people.

Source and Copyright:
The virtue descriptions in this list are the copyright of Peirce Group LLC (https://www.peircegroup.com/). None of the descriptions should be reproduced for any purpose without written permission. Thank you for your Respect for this work.

Virtues Growth

We feel very excited that our virtues can always continue to grow. When something this important grows daily, it becomes a major contributor to our unity and well-being as a couple. We are constantly striving to become our best selves. Virtues differ from our personality traits, which are generally established during our youth and are less likely to be actively developed or changed, although we may occasionally adjust them. [See "Unifier 7: Loving One Another" for some content on personality.]

Here is a perspective on the growth of virtues:

"Cultivation is an apt metaphor for the development of virtue: the best fruits, vegetables, and grains come from strains of plants that have been carefully developed over a long period and that require special treatment to come to fruition. ...Virtues can take root in our lives if we foster them with appropriate care and attention...to become the best people we can be."[10] Blaine Fowers

We notice that the more we acknowledge how our virtue strengths contribute to our relationship and home, the happier we both are and the more loving we feel. We catch each other doing something positive each day, and we express our appreciation. It's like a verbal hug that demonstrates our Positive Spirit and Respect. We become deeply connected. ["Unifier 8: Appreciating One Another", will share more about this.]

Being in a couple relationship provides many signals to us to improve—if we are open to them. It's in the space of our relationship that we often see our behavior triumphs and failures. When we struggle with our own or each other's words or actions, we recognize that we have the choice to improve and build our virtue strengths continually. This is a lifetime process of taking action, reflecting on our words and actions, and improving daily. The next day, our behavior is more powerful, life-enhancing, and beneficial to others.

"In an unconscious partnership, you believe that the way to have a good relationship is to fall in love with the perfect partner. In a conscious partnership, you realize you must be the right partner. As you gain this more realistic view, you acknowledge that creating a good relationship requires commitment, discipline, and the courage to change."[11] Harville Hendrix and Helen LaKelly Hunt

As we recognize that new actions are needed, we can assist each other to grow. For example: One of us may struggle to exhibit a virtue, which is difficult for the other. Perhaps we act negatively when our partner seems mired in a problem or grief over a heartache. We can then strengthen our virtues of Positive Spirit and Compassion in response. This, in turn, encourages the other partner to strengthen a virtue they were not applying, such as Humility or Perseverance. As we see each other apply various virtues, we can be inspired to improve ourselves. While developing our virtues is primarily an individual activity, it's also an ongoing, dynamic process between us.

Demonstrating Trust and Respect prevents us from attacking each other's character virtues or becoming defensive. Character attacks are among the most damaging actions we can do in our relationship, as they wound the heart and soul.

Research has found that:

"... a criticism is global and expresses negative feelings or opinions about the other's character...."[12] John Gottman and Nan Silver

When we are upset with each other, it can be automatic to use angry and critical words. However, it's more effective to initiate consultation about our issues consciously and to focus our attention and words on the positive behaviors and virtues we want to see. [You will learn more about addressing complaints in "Unifier 9: Harmonizing Our Communications".]

Linda Kavelin Popov, author of *The Family Virtues Guide*, along with Dan Popov and John Kavelin, who founded The Virtues Project, discusses the importance of speaking the "Language of the Virtues". Their work with parents and children inspires us as we use Virtue Language with each other as a couple.[13]

Below are examples of character attacks and suggestions for alternative expressions using **Virtue Language**. This is a new language, and it felt strange for us to use it at first. However, as we consistently practice it with one another, we see its powerful, positive effect. More on this language can be found in "Unifier 8: Appreciating One Another".

- *Attack on Dependability:* "You are so irresponsible and always late."
  Virtue Language: "Please use your Dependability and be on time for your appointments."

- *Attack on Justice:* "You are always unfair to me."
  Virtue Language: "Please use your Justice and treat me as your equal partner."

- Attack on Orderliness: "You are very messy."
  Virtue Language: "I request you use your Orderliness and put away the ingredients after cooking."

Sharing from Experience: *"Before we committed to each other, we made sure to know our own and each other's character and virtue strengths and observe each other in real-life circumstances. It's obvious how valuable this was now that we are living together. We both have the strengths of Truthfulness and Trust, and we are very grateful. However, creating a safe space to encourage and influence one another's growth in virtues can be challenging. We must be very kind and tactful so that what we say is perceived as positive encouragement and not criticism. We have also realized how powerful it can be to notice and appreciate each other's efforts to apply virtues in our life together. When we focus more on each other's positive qualities, we demonstrate excellence every day."*

It takes commitment to learn and grow individually and together. Through mutual sharing in our relationship, we can influence and support one another, which contributes to maintaining our love, connection, and unity. This process of gaining gentle feedback from one another about our virtues and actions can then be an ongoing practice. The more we share and consult about our goals, approaches, concerns, and successes, and the more we are connected in this effort, the greater the potential for growth. We are one another's helpmates and partners, and we celebrate our progress together.

Virtue Pairs

Virtues are positive attributes, and when we apply them, we intend to create benefits and positive outcomes. However, we are learning that we can cause harm if we apply a virtue inappropriately, such as to excess, at a poor time, with the wrong person, or in an unwise situation. We often notice that we are most effective when we pair one virtue with a complementary "helper" virtue, as this produces a better and more balanced outcome.

For example, when we pair Compassion with Truthfulness, it protects our unity. We don't speak so frankly with each other that we hurt each other's feelings. As another example, if we want to strengthen our Orderliness, through reorganizing an area of our home, it's wise to use the Quality of Respect to check with our partner first and get their input and agreement.

As we strengthen and encourage each other to consistently practice a full range of virtues, we enhance our ability to function successfully as a unified couple.

Note: If you initially have difficulty turning to each other for encouragement and assistance with virtues growth, you may begin by turning to a close friend or professional instead. Then, you can gradually start turning to each other.

Examples:

In "Unifier 8: Appreciating One Another", you will learn about using Virtue Language for showing appreciation toward one another by including a virtue in the acknowledgement. The examples below demonstrate this practice.

- "I noticed you practiced Self-Discipline and had a great exercise workout this morning. Well done!"
- "Thank you for your Dependability in carrying out our decision to increase unity with your parents. We will have a great meal together."

- "I was happy today that I found our legal paperwork quickly. Your Orderliness has improved so much!"

Applying Virtues:

Interestingly, we can also apply certain virtues to the lifelong process of self-improvement. Below are three possible ones for us to use.

Excellence
- Apply the most appropriate virtue or action to each unique situation rather than doing what we have always done.
- Take advantage of opportunities to improve when they arise and strive to improve every day.
- Hold a high standard of achievement, not settling for "good enough".

Reflection
- Assess words and actions regularly to determine better choices.
- Observe and consider the effect of our words and actions on others.
- Evaluate when to apply more than one virtue simultaneously for a balanced outcome.

Self-Discipline
- Stay with a personal improvement process until achieving a consistent and positive outcome.
- Focus on the beneficial outcome from personal improvements to keep going forward.
- Choose the virtue that's best in each situation rather than the easiest.

Learning Activities:

1. Carefully read the "22 Virtues and Their Descriptions" in the text above. As we read, listen to our internal response to each one. We pay attention to when we have a positive response to seeing a virtue that's generally a strength in one of us, and we appreciate its value in our lives. We might also experience a nudge that points one of us to a virtue that could be strengthened. We may also have personal experiences or cultural views that affect our response to a particular virtue, and we may need to reframe it. (example: The virtue of "Excellence" might seem like it's only a driver for work-related performance. However, we can use Excellence in other parts of our life, such as when creating a happy family.)

2. We each choose a virtue to focus on developing for a mutually agreed-upon length of time. Consult together to generate ideas of specific actions we could take and goals we could set. This may be an effort where using the arts is beneficial. For example, each of us could:

    a. Create a drawing or painting of ourselves and include our strengths and the chosen growth virtue in the picture
    b. Find photos in print publications or online that demonstrate behaviors that reflect specific virtues
    c. Listen to or watch songs, videos, or poems that talk about various virtues, or create a song, video, or poem

3. Below is a form titled "My Virtue Development Plan." This can provide a useful structure for strengthening each chosen virtue and achieving personal accountability. Sometimes, we may prefer applying Orderliness with a

consistent and structured plan, but at other times, we may choose to use Creativity to develop a different or more spontaneous approach. As we each practice our chosen virtues, we will recognize when we successfully apply the virtue to a situation and offer positive affirmation to one another. We promise to celebrate our significant achievements.

My Virtue Development Plan EXAMPLE
Virtue to Develop: Perseverance
Why? Because I often fail to finish my personal projects. Too often, I allow problems or obstacles to discourage me, and I stop being in action. I lose motivation, or I postpone action until "I have more time".
What are the obstacles, barriers, or challenges I face that prevent me from practicing this virtue? I'm experiencing some health difficulties that make me feel tired at times. I'm also reflecting on whether I automatically say "yes" to people, forget to consult with my partner, and don't pause to discern if I have taken on too many personal projects.
Who Can Help or Encourage Me with This? My partner (or friend ____) told me they found some strategies for developing their virtue of Perseverance.
Development Goal (Desired Outcome): I currently observe that I am very distracted and unproductive in my projects. If I could stay consistently focused and in action 75% of the time, I would be practicing Perseverance and completing my projects.

Development Actions:	Start Date:	Assess Date:
1. I will create actionable goals and firm deadlines for when to complete 2 personal growth projects. I will make myself accountable to _____ or someone else for the delivery of these results.	Date	Date
2. Talk with _____ or _____ whenever I feel discouraged; this will help me to address the obstacles so I can keep moving forward.	Date	Date
3. When starting action on each project, I will take a few minutes to reflect on the importance of Perseverance, focus, and determination.	Date	Date
4. Read inspiring quotations and stories about Perseverance daily and visualize myself persevering as I go through my day.	Date	Date
Signs of Improvement: After 1 month of doing this, I completed 1 of the 2 projects, and I'm 75% finished with the second project. I have overcome many challenges that came from my life circumstances and from a couple of difficult interactions with others.		
New Actions to Take: Maintain my accountability and discuss this with my partner (or friend _____) more frequently—at least once every 2 weeks.		

Note: A blank table is provided below for your use, or you can create a similar format on an electronic device or in a notebook.

My Virtue Development Plan (Use whatever format or method works well for you)		
Virtue to Develop:		
Why?		
What are the obstacles, barriers, or challenges I face that prevent me from practicing this Virtue?		
Who Can Help or Encourage Me with This?		
Development Goal (Desired Outcome):		
Development Actions:	**Start Date:**	**Assess Date:**
1.		
2.		
3.		
4.		
Signs of Improvement:		
New Actions to Take:		

Reflection and Consultation:

Throughout this couple guide, there are invitations to practice the virtue of Reflection about your interactions and connection. This practice gives you opportunities to celebrate progress and consult to address issues.

Individuals:

1. What are some virtues that I see as my strengths? What virtues am I assessing in my behavior and focusing on strengthening?
2. What interferes with knowing my virtue strengths and growth areas? How can I overcome these challenges?
3. Which virtues can I apply to enhance my interactions with my relationship partner and other family members?
4. When have I paired two virtues to produce a more positive outcome? Which pairings have been most effective?

Couple:

1. Which virtues do we most appreciate in each other?
2. How does it affect our feelings about each other when we notice and appreciate these virtues?
3. When do we rely on our partner's virtue strengths? When is this positive? When do we rely on our partner instead of developing our own virtue strength?
4. What are beneficial ways for us to influence the growth of each other's virtues?
5. When do we find it difficult to use a virtue strength with each other? What makes it difficult? Would there be benefits from using it anyway?
6. When do we use a virtue strength to excess with each other, and the outcome is poor? Is there another virtue

that could be paired with it to apply Moderation and balance its use?

Section 2:

Creating Shared Values and Vision

Section 2 Introduction

In Section 2, you will begin learning about the Unifiers leading to couple harmony. The three Unifiers in Section 2 lay the foundation for the remaining 17 Unifiers.

As a couple, you form a new entity that has never existed before: your relationship. Even if you have been together for a while, you can "re-create" the quality of your relationship. You empower this process when you use Creativity to develop a vision for what you want and underpin it with the values you both recognize as vital for a thriving relationship.

The priorities you set and the values you hold, as individuals and as a couple, influence your relationship and choices. Your shared vision for your life together influences the direction you're going in and the goals that you set to move you along on your life journey.

In Section 2, you will learn about and apply:

- Unifier 1: Prioritizing Our Relationship
- Unifier 2: What Is Important to Us?
- Unifier 3: Where Are We Going?

Unifier 1: Prioritizing Our Relationship

"Successful couples are on each other's side.
They view themselves as allies, not adversaries."
Susan Page

Focus Statement: We make it a high priority to schedule regular time together as a couple, giving each other our full attention and strengthening our connection and unity.

Deeper Learning:

We are faced with numerous choices about how to spend our time. It's our unified well-being as a couple that we realize we must place at the heart of our agreed-upon choices. We protect the harmony in our relationship as we consistently consider how our choices will affect each other and then choose what is best for both of us. If, instead, we focus only on our self-interests, we can put a wedge between us.

If we become overly involved in commitments and activities that take us away from each other, we can begin to lose a feeling of connection. Disunity and distance can arise. We prevent this from happening through consultation and agreement on the activities beforehand, and after the activity, we come back to each other, deliberately reconnect, and discuss our experiences. It's wise to consult periodically about what we are involved in to see if it's wise to apply Moderation to our time and activity choices, so we have more time together. This assessment can include where our time and skills are most needed and what brings us happiness.

Sharing from Experience: *"We enjoyed doing community service together, and we discovered it was a way to contribute our skills and a strong element that contributed to our unity.*

However, we were asked to do 'one more thing' to benefit our community, and we knew if we said 'yes', it would be too much. We both spent time using Reflection and writing down all we were doing and our motivations for being involved. We considered the time we spent at work and caring for our home. We assessed the impact of our time choices on our relationship and family, and we began to realize that we rarely spent quality time together. We assessed the overall situation and determined to make 'us' a much higher priority. This detailed process helped us feel more in control of our time and choices. We were able to say 'no' to some things, 'yes' to others, and modify yet others. We committed to time together. What a relief!"

We know that it's fine for both of us to have interests that we pursue individually in addition to what we do together. We enjoy watching each other immersed in an activity and hearing the stories afterward. When we experience our partner feeling fulfilled and satisfied, it can also bring us happiness. For example, one of us might create art, participate in a team sport, or act in community theater. Our partner could watch or enjoy the outcome.

Harmonious couple time is a gift to us and those around us, as it contributes to our happiness and love. It's wise to consult and clarify between us what we mean by "couple time". For example, one might think consulting about a child's needs is couple time. The other might think it's only when we go on a social date away from home. The actual activity is less important than whether the time together strengthens our feelings of connection to one another.

Relationship author Susan Page identified in her work the vital practice of couples who consistently demonstrate "goodwill partnership"—a way of positively influencing their relationship. She writes:

"I interviewed thirty-five couples who described themselves as 'thriving.' I thought I might find that they all came from happy, functional families, or that they had unusual degrees of compatibility, or that their problems were relatively minor compared with other couples—none of that was true. Some of them had rotten childhoods and enormous challenges. But there was a quality I found in all of these thriving couples that I find is usually missing in more troubled relationships. I now believe quality is a deeper key to happiness than good communication or mutual respect.

"It's a quality I call a spirit of goodwill. Successful couples are on each other's side. They view themselves as allies, not adversaries. They want to be happy together, and together they make this happen. In a spirit of goodwill, they accept the traits in their partner that they wish were different. They have given up trying to change each other. When they argue, they understand that a different point of view may be valid. Because they want to experience their love all the time, they would rather work toward a solution than hang on stubbornly to their own 'right' point of view."[14] Susan Page

Ahead in "Unifier 3: Where Are We Going?", we will create a vision for our relationship and recognize that achieving our goals will require a significant investment of time. The world is a busy place with many demands on our time. Parenting adds another strong pull on our attention and resources. Distractions and interruptions in daily life are common. However, prioritizing time together vitally supports our individual and relationship well-being.

When we are unified and happy as a couple, it contributes to the security and love our children need, enabling them to grow, learn, and develop in healthy ways. We are also more prepared to be involved in our work and community service. Our unity grows, and we feel more alive and connected.

Examples:

- Have a weekly or monthly date night. [See "Unifier 11: Enjoying Social Time".]
- Enjoy cuddle time on the couch with dessert.
- Train children to allow a few minutes of uninterrupted parents' time each day.
- Organize a nature outing with cooperative challenges.
- Text when away from home with reasonable updates about whereabouts and timing.
- Avoid spending time with others who may tempt us or want us to be unfaithful to each other.

Applying Virtues:

Below are some practical ways to incorporate virtues into daily practices with the theme of this chapter.

Adherence
- Show steadfast faithfulness to each other, respecting our promises or vows of commitment to each other.
- Treat each other's personal information and private activities as confidential.
- Establish clear boundaries and agreements to create a beneficial plan for improving our relationship and achieving long-term success.

Moderation
- Assess the effect of our time choices on our relationship.
- Examine the overall balance of our responsibilities and adjust them as necessary to maintain the unity of our relationship and ensure our well-being.
- Choose to spend leisure time together.

Unity
- Enthusiastically participate in couple activities.
- Focus on increasing sincere harmony while spending time together.
- Identify specific activities that especially increase feelings of connection, appreciation, and long-term commitment.

Learning Activities:

1. Reflect, consult, and agree on times and activities when mobile phones are turned off or silenced and not responded to. Agree on what could qualify as an acceptable interruption we would respond to.

2. Consult on ways to maintain regular contact with each other when apart and try them. Afterward, assess and agree on what was effective and what we commit to continuing to do.

3. Identify an area or activity where we could be more allied with each other and carry out the steps needed to increase unity and goodwill partnership.

4. Plan a time away from home for intimate conversations about wishes and dreams.

Couple Reflection and Consultation:

Throughout this guide, there are invitations to practice the virtue of Reflection about your interactions and connection. This practice gives you opportunities to celebrate progress and consult to address issues.

1. How can we know if something is good for us?
2. When have we been effective at having a spirit of goodwill in our relationship? How does having this spirit contribute to the thriving of our relationship?
3. How could we increase our spirit of goodwill toward one another? How could this benefit us?
4. When is it wise to suspend judgment about each other and fact-find, so we don't overreact?
5. How do we perceive being in communication with each other when we are apart? How can using Respect influence our choices with this?
6. How can we protect our relationship from harm?
7. How happy or unhappy are we with the amount of couple time we have? What do we want to do differently?
8. Does our current time together feel like quality time? Why or why not? Are there new approaches to try?
9. How does time on our electronic devices affect our quality time as a couple? What is beneficial? What seems potentially harmful? What boundaries or practices would we now like to incorporate into our lives?
10. Are we balancing who does the arranging of couple time? If not, what new arrangements need to be made?
11. How do we feel about watching or hearing about each other's activities or accomplishments?
12. When does spending time with family members also feel like quality time together? When doesn't it?

13. When does spending time with friends also feel like couple time? When doesn't it?

Unifier 2: What Is Important to Us?

*"We cannot say enough about the importance of
staying true to your deepest values and
of honoring those of your partner."*
Patricia Love and Steven Stosny

Focus Statement: We are aware of our own and each other's high-priority values, and we co-create shared values for our relationship and life together.

Deeper Learning:

Values drive the prioritizing of our time and the reasons for our actions. As partners, we grow by exploring our perspectives and beliefs, and then we form a shared foundation of what is important to us and the outcomes we want to achieve in our lives. This shared foundation demonstrates the unity referred to in "Core Element A: Commitment to Unity."

When something is important to us, we use our Honor and dedicate our time to accomplishing it. For example, if family unity is an essential principle for us, we make a point to spend time with our children and other relatives regularly. If we value our work or education, then this is a significant way we spend our time. If contributing to the lives of others is something we value, we engage in various types of community service. If we are motivated by personal growth, spiritual enrichment, and worship, then spiritually based activities are essential to us. If we value nature and enjoy being outdoors, we spend time there and perhaps live close to a natural environment. If we have ethnic or cultural heritages that we identify with and want to incorporate into our life, we will carry out various celebrations, ceremonies, or traditions.

If entertainment is a priority, we may choose to spend our time watching television or movies, attending concerts, playing games, and so on. Perhaps physical fitness is a priority, and we exercise regularly. Social media may be another way we spend our time, and we use it to connect with others. However, we stay aware when social media and electronic device use is excessive and becomes a barrier between us.

Sharing from Experience: *"We were both regular exercisers when we began dating. One swam a lot, and the other did muscle-strengthening at the gym and rode a bike. We tried exercising together, but it didn't seem to work well. Our bodies needed different activities, and our schedules did not mesh well for exercising. After committing to a life together, we both enjoy going on walks, which is good exercise and a great opportunity to spend time talking together. However, we generally still do serious exercise separately. We promised each other that we would do our best to accomplish some form of exercise daily and let the other know about it. We don't meet this goal 100%, but the promise keeps us motivated to exercise and encourages each other. We congratulate each other on our achievements. We value being active throughout our lives."*

We gain insights when we use Reflection to examine our core values and consider how they impact our use of time and energy. We sometimes discover discrepancies between what we identify as our core values and where we spend most of our time. For example, we may claim to value quality time with each other, but then we respond to work emails and calls during evenings and weekends instead of truly connecting. When we have values in common, it can be easier to determine our choices and what we see as a larger purpose for our lives. When we have diverging values, we can sometimes experience conflict or disappointment.

Here is a perspective on the link between values and commitments:

"Every time we make and keep a commitment to ourselves—large or small—we increase our self-confidence. We build our reserves. We enlarge our capacity to make and keep greater commitments, both to ourselves and to others. ... [W]hen keeping your commitment becomes hard, you have two choices: You can change your behavior to match your commitment, or you can lower your values to match your behavior. One choice will strengthen your integrity; the other will diminish it and erode your confidence in your ability to make and keep commitments in the future. In addition, that shift in direction with regard to values—even if it's slight—will create a change in trajectory that will create a far more significant difference in destination down the road."[15] Stephen M. R. Covey

As we reflect on our values, we will see whether our behaviors show that we value each other and our relationship. Do we stay in regular communication? Do we enjoy spending time together? Do we demonstrate Respect in our interactions? We reflect on this:

"... [T]here are a few rules I know to be true about love and marriage: If you don't respect the other person, you're gonna have a lot of trouble. If you don't know how to compromise, you're gonna have a lot of trouble. If you can't talk openly about what goes on between you, you're gonna have a lot of trouble. And if you don't have a common set of values in life, you're gonna have a lot of trouble. Your values must be alike."[16] Morrie Schwartz

When we value our relationship, we believe meeting each other's needs thoughtfully and to the best of our ability is essential. Demonstrating Service to each other can be a vital contributor to our thriving relationship. We consider what each other needs to be happy and healthy, and we strive to carry out the words and actions that contribute to well-being to the best of our ability. We recognize that these needs will vary according to the stage of our relationship, family composition, and unique circumstances. [See "Unifier 13: Giving Thoughtful Service".]

Our shared values keep our words and behaviors in line with what is important to us:

> "Every time you violate your core values—even if you're just reacting to your partner—you feel guilty. For example, if one of your core values is to be a loving partner and you forget your anniversary, you'll feel guilty. Guilt is the direct result of your beliefs and actions being out of alignment with each other. It's your brain's way of warning you to get back in line with your core values. ... We cannot say enough about the importance of staying true to your deepest values and honoring your partner's. If you make this a regular practice, your relationship will improve and be transformed without ever talking about it."[17] Patricia Love and Steven Stosny

Note: You will find more on the concepts covered in this Unifier in "Section 4: Creating Connecting Experiences".

Examples:

- "We value being fit and living a long life, so we exercise regularly."

- "We value our couple and family unity, so we apply Moderation to our time choices with work, leisure activities, and community service, and we spend quality time at home."
- "We value ongoing learning, so we both read books and take courses, sometimes together."

Applying Virtues:

Below are some practical ways to incorporate virtues into daily practices with the theme of this chapter.

Dependability
- Keep promises to each other in a timely manner, utilizing our virtue of Trust and fostering harmony.
- Align our actions with our shared values.
- Hold fast to and remain faithful to our values with courage and conviction, even in the face of pressure, challenge, or temptation.

Honor
- Identify, understand, and appreciate each other's values and how they connect to our shared values.
- Consult and agree on our shared values.
- Actively apply shared values in daily actions, choices, and decisions.

Purposefulness
- Identify long-term goals that are consistent with our shared values.
- Focus on activities that contribute to achieving our long-term goals.
- Courageously apply our highest values in using and sacrificing our time and energy for positive purposes.

Learning Activities:

1. Individually, list our top five values that underpin our time choices. Share our lists and consult with each other about how these values affect our lives individually and together. Consult on whether to adjust our time management approach and what new actions we commit to.

2. Write a list together of the values that we want to be at the foundation of our relationship. Consult about how these values might influence our daily choices. If we have children who can participate, consult as a family about our foundational values.

3. Choose one of our values and create a list of ways to spend time together to bring it to life.

Couple Reflection and Consultation:

Throughout this couple guide, there are invitations to practice the virtue of Reflection about your interactions and connection. This practice gives you opportunities to celebrate progress and consult to address issues.

1. How can clear individual and shared values contribute to our life together?
2. How can we determine core values that apply to our relationship? To our family?
3. Who else could assist us with clarifying our values?
4. How can we remember and apply our values when faced with a situation or decision?

Unifier 3: Where Are We Going?

"Putting your whole heart into a relationship
is the only way to get maximum value from it."
George S. Pransky

Focus Statement: Our values support and harmonize our vision for our lives together, and this vision provides a broader perspective on where we commit to going in our relationship and life choices.

Deeper Learning:

We contribute to creating our relationship together when we agree on our vision and base it on the values we identified in "Unifier 2: What Is Important to Us?". It can be easy to carry out the day-to-day tasks of life and not see our destination. Developing a vision reminds us to lift our eyes and see a larger life plan. We can look ahead and see the potential fruits of our efforts.

Many future-looking questions occur to us as we consider our vision, such as:

- When we picture our couple life, what do we want to see?
- What do we want to create together?
- What do we want our relationship to be like?
- Are we going to raise children?
- What values and virtues do we want our children to learn?
- Where do we choose to live?
- What type of home environment and atmosphere do we find attractive?
- What are we striving for in terms of material well-being?

- What do we want to achieve with our self-expression and Creativity, and how can this be accommodated in our relationship?
- How can spiritual elements enhance our lives? What daily habits will we incorporate?

We may be tempted to focus on: "What do we *not* want?". However, it's wise for us to focus on the positive we want to create instead. We must also consider what is changing in our lives, what needs may have shifted, and what is essential for us to prioritize.

Change and individual differences affect all relationships:

"Throughout the marriage husband and wife must make room—even if reluctantly—for change and for difference, for altering values, tastes, needs, and careers. Husband and wife continually confront the issue of how to reshape their shared identity so it continues to express what they want as a couple and what they need as individuals. Given the vast number of choices and trajectories, this challenge creates a never-ending tension in marriage.

"... [I]t is out of this push-pull of autonomy and togetherness that the couple acquires a sense of good emotional, moral, and cognitive fit. To reach the conclusion that the relationship is uniquely gratifying requires the meshing of both partners' conscious and unconscious wishes and needs and the acceptance of compromise as reasonably fair or at least temporarily necessary. To achieve this state, not only must each person feel free to make his or her wishes known but both must agree on what is fair."[18] Judith S. Wallerstein and Sandra Blakeslee

Note: For more content on fair partnership, refer to "Unifier 6: Respecting Each Other".

We have tremendous power and latitude in using Creativity to develop a shared couple identity and determine our vision. We are creating something new in the world that *has never existed before.* As a couple striving for unity, our relationship is increasingly greater than the sum of the two of us as individuals.

Sharing from Experience: *"When we were deciding whether to be lifetime partners, we consulted on what we wanted our relationship to be like and what practical actions we could take to achieve that vision. When we realized we were in harmony with our vision and the commitments we were willing to make, it became a powerful confirmation that we could confidently move forward. Now, we revisit our vision and actions every few months and celebrate when we fulfill our commitments. We also note where we are not progressing toward our vision and what changes we want to make to get there."*

Using words to state what we are committed to creating or re-creating is powerful. We can focus specifically on what is important to both of us and consider the vital practices that will assist our relationship to thrive. The more specific we are in stating what we want to create and in clarifying the actions we commit to carrying out, the more we will discover our shared vision and priorities. *This visioning process must not include blaming or criticizing each other for what has or hasn't happened in the past!*

It takes commitment to fulfill our vision. We stay in our relationship through all its joys and challenges. Keeping this commitment to practice Perseverance involves time, focus, and sacrifice. We commit to ourselves to stay, and we commit to the other person to be there, almost no matter what happens, good or bad. Demonstrating Adherence enables us to maintain our promises and vows to each other. Commitment drives us to take action and create a strong, happy, and united couple relationship.

Below are some perspectives on commitment that provide us with perspectives about its necessity.

"The benefit you get from commitment is peace of mind on both sides. Your partner benefits from knowing you are committed to maintain respect and affinity. He [and She] need not fear that circumstance and personal reactions will hurt the relationship. It is human nature for our degree of satisfaction to be tied to the extent of our involvement. Commitment prepares the mind for full involvement and guards against distractions. Putting your whole heart into a relationship is the only way to get maximum value from it. Commitment to a relationship enables you to experience its full potential."[19] George S. Pransky

"Until one is committed there is hesitancy, the chance to draw back, always ineffectiveness. Concerning all acts of initiative (and creation), there is one elementary truth, the ignorance of which kills countless ideas and splendid plans: that the moment one definitely commits oneself, then Providence moves too. All sorts of things occur to help one that would never otherwise have occurred. A whole stream of events issues from the decision, raising in one's favor all manner of unforeseen incidents and meetings and material assistance...."[20] W. H. Murray

Once we clearly state our vision, we expand it to include statements of our commitments that will fulfill it. These, in turn, guide us when we make choices and decisions. For instance, if we commit to spending time in community service activities, we may choose to forgo another activity and volunteer time with a charitable organization instead. If we are experiencing a conflict, we can examine whether there's a virtue or commitment we are not fulfilling with each other or other people. Re-starting what is missing can restore harmony and prevent annoyances and larger disagreements. In other words, striving to fulfill our vision and accomplish our commitments creates unity, as we learned in "Core Element A: Commitment to Unity".

For example, we might write down that we are committed to consulting as a couple at least once a week, more often when possible. Fulfilling this commitment then releases positive energy into our relationship. It's generally harder to criticize or fight with someone when we regularly strive to create unified outcomes. [See "Core Element B: Reflection and Consultation" for more about this.]

As challenges come up throughout our life, we can lift our eyes and remind ourselves of the vision we want to fulfill. When we refer to our written commitments, it empowers us to take positive action. When we are tired, the car has mechanical problems, the bills are due, we disagree about who will clean the bathroom, the children are annoying each other, and it all seems too much, re-focusing on our commitments can restore some of our balance. They remind us of what is most important to both of us, and when we look at them, it prompts us to resume some of the beneficial actions we may have stopped doing.

As we strive to clarify our vision and fulfill our commitments, we will reaffirm that our relationship is a strong and viable entity. Even if we have been together for a while and are experiencing difficulties, we can begin anew.

Applying Virtues:

Below are some practical ways to incorporate virtues into daily practices with the theme of this chapter.

Creativity
- Generate and consider new ideas to incorporate into our vision and commitments.
- Carry out our vision in unique ways.
- Develop visible displays related to our vision.

Excellence
- Reflect and learn from our experiences.
- Stretch our lives to achieve higher goals and our vision.
- Assess our commitments for fairness and rebalance as needed.

Purposefulness
- Assess our progress regularly using our vision and commitments and re-align our actions as needed.
- Set goals and measurements to keep us moving forward toward our long-term vision.
- Determine a regular interval to reflect on and assess our progress.

Learning Activities:

1. Create a vision statement for our relationship that clearly articulates our values and what we aim to achieve. At this stage, we may have identified items we want to write down, but we will allow the ideas to flow over a few weeks while we study the rest of the Unifiers.

2. Create a vision board, which is a collage of pictures and words from various sources or personal photographs that depict what we want in our life together and for our short- or long-term goals. Visually seeing our goals and desires every day, consciously and subconsciously supports us in achieving them.

3. Consult about and write down the action-oriented commitments that will assist us in fulfilling our vision. Keep adding to them and refining them as we study.

4. Draw a map on a large piece of paper or cardboard and mark the landmarks on it that illustrate our relationship goals.

Couple Reflection and Consultation:

Throughout this couple guide, there are invitations to practice the virtue of Reflection about your interactions and connection. This practice gives you opportunities to celebrate progress and consult to address issues.

1. What elements do we envision as essential for a long-term and happy partnership?
2. What habits or practices have we observed in other couples that seem attractive and beneficial for us to adopt?
3. Are there any dreams or wishes we want to include in our vision, even if we don't know how to achieve them yet?
4. When we talk about "thriving", what does that look like to us?
5. What will assist us in keeping our vision visible? Keep us actively engaged in fulfilling its elements?

6. What system will prompt us to periodically review, reflect, and consult about our vision?
7. What value do we see in having action-oriented commitments that align with our vision?
8. Are there others who can provide input on our vision and commitments?

Section 3:

Creating a Loving Partnership

Section 3 Introduction

Loving partnerships that show you cherish each other and practice Respect with one another have unique aspects for every couple. Together, you will create ways to maintain your friendship, build understanding, and express love to one another, all of which will increase your unity. You will learn about each other's preferred ways of receiving love and practice expressing love in those ways. Demonstrating understanding, appreciation, and love powerfully through your words and actions keeps you connected.

You will draw closer together by developing a partnership between the two of you. Being partners means you're equal in your interactions, collaborative in your endeavors, and united in your loyalty to each other.

In Section 3, you will learn more about these Unifiers and ways to apply them:

- Unifier 4: Establishing Our Friendship
- Unifier 5: Understanding Each Other
- Unifier 6: Respecting Each Other
- Unifier 7: Loving One Another
- Unifier 8: Appreciating One Another
- Unifier 9: Harmonizing Our Communications

Unifier 4: Establishing Our Friendship

*"A happy spouse looks at the other person as
their best and closest friend—a friend they want to
stay close to no matter what."*
Shaunti Feldhahn

Focus Statement: We consider each other a close friend, valuing our sincere loyalty, open communication, shared laughter, and mutual support.

Deeper Learning:

A deep friendship is essential to a high-quality, thriving, and lasting relationship. Therefore, we are committed to the belief that friendship is a key contributor to our unity. Using our Honor guides us to keep our friendship strong and healthy.

Sharing many experiences and activities and having forged a high-quality connection between us demonstrates that we are friends. Our friendship and intimacy deepen and strengthen over time, forming a lasting foundation for us as a couple.

Being friends means connecting, sharing, and caring about one another. We are in each other's corner, looking out for each other, and sharing most aspects of our lives. We feel safe together, so we can use our Trust to be vulnerable with each other. We are in one long conversation as close friends and companions. We share positive experiences that create lasting memories. We increase intimacy as we connect body, mind, heart, and soul.

Sharing from Experience: *"Friendship and liking each other set the foundation for us to enjoy each other. Friendship helps us communicate and feel drawn to spend time together. We enjoy* *practicing Service with each other and others around us, and we work toward common goals. We honestly share what we are thinking and feeling. We laugh and have fun together. Our shared history as friends helps us feel connected."*

Scientific studies support the emphasis on being close friends:

"... [H]appy marriages are based on a deep friendship. By this I mean a mutual respect for and enjoyment of each other's company. These couples tend to know each other intimately—they are well versed in each other's likes, dislikes, personality quirks, hopes, and dreams. They have an abiding regard for each other and express this fondness not just in the big ways but through small gestures day in and day out. ... Friendship fuels the flames of romance because it offers the best protection against feeling adversarial toward your spouse. ... In the strongest marriages, husband and wife share a deep sense of meaning. They don't just 'get along'—they also support each other's hopes and aspirations and build a sense of purpose into their lives together."[21] John M. Gottman and Nan Silver

"It turns out, happy couples hang out. Either consciously or subconsciously, they work to maintain their friendship rather than take it for granted. And the most important way they do that is to spend time together. They are in proximity to each other a lot. ... A happy spouse looks at the other person as their best and closest friend—a friend they want to stay close to no matter what."[22] Shaunti Feldhahn

Maintaining our friendship isn't always easy—it takes commitment, time, attention, and love. Being a steadfast and loyal friend to one another requires patience and the ability to understand, forgive, and move past unpleasantness or disagreements. It also acknowledges that friendships and relationships go through ups and downs, so there's not just one way for us to interact.

Being friends is one of the best ways for us to feel a strong connection with each other. Consider these perspectives:

"A simple way to understand connection is to think of it as two people sharing an experience. You touch me, I feel your touch. You talk, I listen, and vice versa. Individuals make connection by paying attention and tuning in to one another—as well as what they are doing. It's as if for a moment there are no barriers between you. Each has access to the other's energy, which creates synergy and intensifies the experience."[23] Patricia Love

"We discovered that when we help couples change their interactive behaviors—rather than how they feel, think, or remember—they feel connected and begin to have new thoughts and create new memories."[24] Harville Hendrix and Helen LaKelly

Sharing from Experience: *"Being friends provides a mindset that enables us to cultivate well-being and form a defense against the harshness in the world around us. We are a safe space for each other to relax."*

Examples:

- Excitedly share about a work accomplishment and respond with enthusiasm.

- Encourage and celebrate each other's progress on difficult tasks.
- Cook a meal while the other is visiting a sick relative, so it's ready when they come home.
- Bring home a book or story that the other would find interesting.
- Share an inspirational video or article.
- Talk about a hope, wish, or dream we have and make plans to achieve it.

Applying Virtues:

Below are some practical ways to incorporate virtues into daily practices with the theme of this chapter.

Politeness and Sociability
- Enjoy time together doing nothing and everything, including relaxation time in the mix.
- Use courteous manners with one another, remembering to use words such as "please" and "thank you".
- Greet each other with warm and welcoming smiles and hugs.

Honor
- Hold strongly to loyalty in words and actions.
- Look for and appreciate the best in each other.
- Believe in each other's goodwill and integrity.

Trust
- Count on each other to respond when needed.
- Believe we are demonstrating Truthfulness with our words and actions.

- Accompany each other through good times and difficult ones.

Learning Activities:

1. Reflect and consult on our strengths and areas for growth to maintain the quality of our friendship. Consider some of these aspects:

   a. Carrying out kind and honest communications
   b. Enjoying quiet, peaceful time together
   c. Engaging in play, fun, and laughter
   d. Feeling free to be ourselves
   e. Learning about each other
   f. Enthusiastically supporting what is best for each other
   g. Encouraging each other
   h. Staying loyal
   i. Maintaining Trust and Dependability
   j. Sharing interests
   k. Creating common experiences and positive memories

2. Each of us shares a brief story about how a friendship has positively contributed to our lives as individuals or how a friend is currently benefiting our shared life.

3. Create a new relaxation activity that encourages us to feel at home and peaceful with one another.

Couple Reflection and Consultation:

Throughout this couple guide, there are invitations to practice the virtue of Reflection about your interactions and connection. This practice gives you opportunities to celebrate progress and consult to address issues.

1. What indicates that we are both friends and partners?
2. How does being friends assist us through difficulties?
3. What encourages us to relax with each other?
4. How do we feel and respond when we are in an activity that prompts laughter and enjoyment?
5. What prompts each of us to laugh?
6. How do we feel about having fun?
7. How does being friends positively influence our relationships with others?
8. What could enhance our friendship?

Unifier 5: Understanding Each Other

"...[E]motionally intelligent couples
are intimately familiar with each other's world."
John M. Gottman and Nan Silver

Focus Statement: We strive to pay attention, share, listen, encourage, and understand each other's thoughts and feelings with care and patience.

Deeper Learning:

We feel unified when we share our inner worlds, listen to one another, and inquire about each other's viewpoints on matters that arise. This keeps us current with what is happening with each other and assists us to hear and understand the mysteries in each other's hearts and minds. We have opportunities to address emotional and practical issues and encourage one another's activities and dreams. All of this increases emotional intimacy:

"... [E]motionally intelligent couples are intimately familiar with each other's world. ... They remember the major events in each other's history, and they keep updating their information as the facts and feelings of their spouse's world change. ... Couples who have detailed love maps of each other's world are far better prepared to cope with stressful events and conflict."[25] John M. Gottman and Nan Silver

We know we are each at a different stage of developing the skills to achieve emotional intelligence about one another. We have observed that women tend to be more comfortable with this type of interaction. However, we have also noticed that men are acquiring the necessary skills, so we are confident that we can continue to improve in this area.

Sharing and Listening

We notice that our communications go more smoothly when we are clear at the beginning about our goals or expectations. Sometimes, we want to consult to solve an issue. At other times, we only want someone to listen to us and empathize. Often, we can then process and understand an issue emotionally. Either way, we appreciate it when our partner listens, summarizes, and asks clarifying questions. These practices build understanding and demonstrate Respect. We feel relaxed, confident, validated, and connected when we know we have been heard.

With effective listening, we gain a greater understanding of what is happening with each other. As we share and listen, we improve the quality of our friendship, intimacy, and unity. Conscious listening, as described below, contributes to effective consultation and problem-solving, which then reduces or prevents conflicts between us.

Below are three levels of conscious listening:

- *Level One:* Listen for content—Be able to give a concise and accurate summary of what we heard the speaker say.
- *Level Two:* Listen for the emotions—Be able to hear the emotion under the words of the speaker.
- *Level Three:* Listen for the speaker's wants and needs—Be able to hear beneath the words and the emotions what the speaker is asking for and needing.[26] Summarized from Kathlyn Hendricks and Gay Hendricks

Of course, it's also beneficial when the speaker can articulate their emotions, wants, and needs. With our close relationship, we often have a greater sensitivity to one another's thoughts and feelings. Occasionally, we can guess what our partner thinks, feels, wants, or needs. However, making assumptions without directly asking and listening to determine what is happening is unwise. We can get upset when the other doesn't "read our mind" and, therefore, know what to do for us. However, we recognize that the ability to read minds accurately is a myth, and the best principle for us to apply is to use communication and consultation to discover the truth.

Virtues such as Self-Discipline and Compassion influence our effectiveness as listeners. Strengthening these virtues reduces disruption in the process and enables us to better see the topic from our partner's point of view. We stay consciously focused on listening and understanding rather than trying to plan our response or strategize how to fix the problem. We also achieve the best outcomes when we avoid competing verbally and refrain from interrupting.

It takes practice, mutual encouragement, and genuine care to stay tuned in to each other's inner world. Taking the time to do focused listening is a way to practice Respect. We focus better when we set aside what we are doing and eliminate distractions, such as those from our electronic devices. When we tune in to what our partner shares, we align our thoughts and feelings and understand one another more deeply.

Understanding Feelings

It contributes to our friendship and the quality of our consultations when we share our feelings and strive to understand each other's emotions. They influence how we:

- Perceive the situation we are addressing
- Express our thoughts

- Make decisions
- Create and carry out possible solutions

We improve our life together and reduce conflict by increasing our skills with the factors listed below.

- Stay aware of our current and underlying thoughts and feelings
- Understand what has prompted our feelings, including differentiating between whether it was something from the past, the present, or a mix of both
- Maintain self-control and adjust, not letting feelings be in charge instead of us
- Be able to express intense thoughts and feelings calmly, clearly, and safely, releasing or calming them through such activities as quiet use of Reflection and prayer, or through constructive physical action
- Understand each other's thoughts and feelings through mutual sharing, and listen patiently throughout so there's space to learn
- Apply Compassion for each other's feelings

Here are some thoughts about how to process feelings:

"… [R]epressed or suppressed feelings have damaging impact on your health and well-being and this often drives people into counseling or therapy, or they simply fester in unresolved, unhappy, health- and relationship-damaging ways. …

"What does 'processing your feelings' mean? It means experiencing them, bringing them into conscious awareness so you can feel them, look at them, explore them, think them over, realize insights about them, release them…any or all of the above, wherever the process takes you. When people experience their feelings in these kinds of ways, they lose their punch. Feelings are transitory by nature. They come…and they go…IF you allow yourself to experience them. But, if you tell yourself any kind of message that blocks your feelings or causes them to get pushed away, they will keep popping up one way or another to grab your attention, sometimes at inopportune times or in inopportune ways. Telling yourself 'I shouldn't feel that way', or, 'I'm carrying on too much about this', or 'I'm being too sensitive', or even, 'Not now' seriously impedes your ability to experience your feelings and may, ultimately, make it difficult to access those feelings.

"… [I]f you deny or push aside Feeling A, it's likely to have a negative impact on Feeling B. This is because denial is a primitive coping mechanism, which means that it doesn't simply target the one feeling you want to block off, or lessen, it causes collateral damage to others. So, if you want to have access to happiness and joy and other 'good stuff'…open the door to feeling the tough stuff like loss, sadness, hurt, fear, loneliness, pain, despair.

"So, how do you open the door to experiencing your feelings? The key to giving yourself full access to them is to forgo labeling them as 'good' or 'bad', or otherwise pushing them around in any way: Let them simply be."[27]
Patty Howell

Generally, the quality of our consultations improves when we acknowledge and share our thoughts and feelings about a topic early in the process. Expressing feelings doesn't mean attacking each other with anger or any other emotion. It does mean saying what feelings are happening and why, so understanding builds between us.

We benefit from recognizing shifting feelings in ourselves and each other as new conversations arise or when situations change. Disunity can occur when we don't acknowledge each other's feelings, devalue them, or remain silent and withdrawn for an extended period. Withholding feelings or thoughts and speaking up later when it's too late to address an issue usually causes frustration and problems. This could include saying things like, "Well, I didn't think that idea would work," or "I felt uneasy about that action" after it occurred.

We remember from reading "Core Element B: Reflection and Consultation" that sharing our feelings and striving for understanding are different than our feelings clashing with each other and conflict escalating. A simple practice can be for one of us to say, "I'm wondering how you're feeling about this situation? Can you share with me what is on your mind and heart?". We must say this with an accepting tone of voice, without accusation or judgment, and then allow silence to invite a response. A follow-up practice after speaking can be for the listener to ask, "Is there anything else you need to say?" This ensures our partner's inner cup empties. We may need to stop at times and summarize back to each other what we think we have heard. When we check for understanding, we quickly correct information and let each other know we are listening carefully.

Often, one or both of us may need time and space alone to allow feelings to surface and clarify. When we struggle to identify our feelings, it can be helpful to write down an incident or situation and then list the associated feelings, either privately in a journal or with the assistance of another person.

However, one challenge with understanding feelings is that we may not yet be skillful with the words to label them. Dr. Marshall B. Rosenberg, in his materials on non-violent communication, guides people through the challenges of understanding and identifying feelings. He encourages specificity, which has us state that we are "happy", "excited", or "relieved", rather than saying we feel "good". Being specific contributes to our understanding and clarity.

Some of the words we might use for our feelings when our needs are *being met* are:

- Adventurous
- Affectionate
- Amazed
- Amused
- Aroused
- Calm
- Curious
- Energetic
- Fascinated

- Happy
- Mellow
- Moved
- Optimistic
- Proud
- Relaxed
- Surprised
- Thrilled
- Wonderful

Some of the words for our feelings when our needs are *not being met* are:

- Afraid
- Angry
- Annoyed
- Anxious
- Ashamed
- Bored
- Concerned
- Confused
- Disappointed

- Discouraged
- Embarrassed
- Hurt
- Irritated
- Jealous
- Overwhelmed
- Pessimistic
- Resentful
- Sad[28]

Marshall B. Rosenberg

Sharing Our Feelings

With practice, we may be able to identify and name our feelings quickly, or sometimes do so with assistance.

Alternatively, we may notice that our feelings become clearer to ourselves when we share during consultation. We may easily and intuitively identify feelings, or we may need gentle, exploratory, and curious questions to sort them out. It's wise for us to avoid making assumptions or judgments about each other and to inquire and acknowledge how each feels. It's unwise, and we may end up frustrated or arguing if we:

- Tell our partner how they are feeling
- Project our feelings onto our partner
- Tell our partner that they should or should not have a certain feeling
- Judge and criticize our partner for having the feeling

Our vocal volumes, tones of voice, facial expressions, and body movements are powerful cues about our thoughts and feelings. If we pay close attention, we can begin to observe our own feelings. If we listen carefully, we can often tell if our partner is upset, happy, angry, excited, or annoyed. When someone's words, facial expressions, body movements, and tone of voice don't align, we will likely believe their tone. It's wise to fact-check what we notice by asking gentle questions.

As we become more skillful in aligning our feelings and words, our practice of Trust strengthens. It's then easier to offer one another gentle feedback and communicate effectively about our concerns.

How we express and understand each other's feelings can also be influenced by cultural factors or regional accents. Our unique personalities may also affect how we express our feelings, leading to misunderstandings.

Exploring all these factors together during a calm time may uncover and resolve issues that are causing us problems.

Sharing from Experience: *"Over the years, there are many ways we non-verbally communicate our love and affection—a look, a smile, a touch—even when with friends. We have learned that the tone of our voice can communicate more than the words we say when we are disgruntled, anxious, frustrated, or unhappy. We have discovered that it's better to consult about an issue when we are in a positive frame of mind. If we are in a negative state, those feelings color the issue. That also gives us time to pray, reflect, and consider options."*

At times, what is happening emotionally with us has nothing to do with our partner but instead relates to other events in our lives. Tuning into our feelings and their cause can prompt us to communicate that our partner isn't the source, and then we can both relax a bit. Perhaps a neighbor's accident causes some grief related to a family member dying in an accident in the past. Maybe a clerk was rude in a store, and anger is simmering. Something happened at work, and there's a fear of job loss. We can listen to each other, so we understand our feelings better and let them calm down.

When the feelings that arise are between the two of us instead, it's often more challenging to handle them well. We need to keep practicing so that we can convey our feelings in a constructive way that doesn't hurt each other. When we suppress our feelings until we think it's the right time, they can begin to leak out in unclear ways that confuse our partner. They could also pile up and become an ugly mess when they do come out. It may be useful to request a consultation or to schedule a routine time each day or each week to check in and address any issues that have arisen. However, there are times when issues arise and must be addressed immediately.

Sharing from Experience: *"When we speak, we are aware of how our words include the idea we are trying to convey and* how we feel about it. With this awareness, we take time to speak as skillfully as possible, while we also have confidence that our partner will listen attentively. We speak our minds, and we let go of what we have said.

"As we listen proactively, we are aware of our internal reactions, arising thoughts, and feelings. However, we also know that the process of consulting allows time and space for us to share what each of us feels is needed and helpful. This allows our minds to stay relatively quiet while the other speaks. We can truly hear what is being said as we consider our own opinions and formulate a response.

"Our consultation is then a process of being aware of our feelings as we speak and as we listen. There's a sense of great support in knowing that our marriage partner is openly aware as we do this. For example, I recently returned home from a week-long business trip. My wife was exhausted from caring for our sick four-year-old son for three days.

"When we had a few minutes to sit and catch up with each other and consult about what would happen the next day, we needed time to share our feelings. My wife said, 'I was very scared I was going to have to take him to the hospital without you here'. She added, 'I was so upset that you didn't call last night to check on us.'

"With mindful listening, I was able to acknowledge her feelings of loneliness and fear about handling this challenge on her own, without jumping into being defensive. She could then hear me as I shared, 'I was very frustrated that there was no cell phone signal along the route we were driving last night.' I went on to say, 'I was very concerned about both of you and hoped you could feel my prayer support'.

"Listening to each other's feelings helped us reconnect. We also realized that we were both too tired to consult about plans for the next day. All we needed right then was to agree on how to care for our son for the next few hours."

In this story, the couple was effective because they were able to share their feelings without interruption. Each was able to listen without immediate judgment. Each was detached enough to realize that they would have to continue the consultation later when they were less tired.

When we reflect and consult about our feelings, here are some steps that we find useful to follow:

1. Acknowledge and name the feelings we are experiencing
2. Determine what has likely caused the feelings
3. Assess or consult about what to do about the feelings using questions like these:

   a. Is there a problem? Do we need to address it with someone?
   b. Are the feelings coming from an old situation, and once recognized that they are not part of the present circumstances, can they be released?
   c. Is there physical activity to do that will release and calm the feeling, so it's easier to think about it and address it?
   d. Do we need to give ourselves some time to understand what we are feeling and why?
   e. Is the feeling causing harm to us or other people?
   f. Is the feeling brief and temporary, or has it been with us for a while and needs help from others?
   g. What actions should be taken?

We must apply Perseverance when consulting with each other. We take the time to understand each other, increase our emotional intimacy, and grow our unity. Understanding then becomes part of the culture of our partnership:

"When a spouse accurately understands their partner's situation, feelings, and motives, conflicts are curbed. Intimacy increases. Misunderstandings are few and far between. Two people who read each other well, who are enjoying mutual empathy, have more laughter and less bickering. They offer more care and comfort. They have fewer hurt feelings and more fun. They are less judgmental and more perceptive. They indulge each other's quirks. They find more patience for one another. More forgiveness. An abundance of grace and gratitude. In short, more love."[29] Les and Leslie Parrott and David H. Olson

Note: Additional information on understanding your personalities, expressing love, and providing emotional support is in "Unifier 7: Loving One Another". Additional information on communication is in "Unifier 9: Harmonizing Our Communications".

Caution: It's essential to seek help when your feelings and interactions are causing significant distress and remain unresolved. There's a difference between feelings that arise normally every day, or you have an occasional annoying interaction, rather than when the emotions are deep, serious, and stay for long periods. These are likely best addressed with a mental health professional.

Examples:

- Share about needing to go on a vacation.
- Explain the challenges occurring in starting a new job, project, or task.
- Express concerns about a child.
- Share grief about a loss.
- Show concern about each other's well-being.

- Understand that something from the past is being triggered in one or both of us, and agree to focus on the present situation instead.

Applying Virtues:

Below are some practical ways to incorporate virtues into daily practices with the theme of this chapter.

Compassion
- Pay close attention to nonverbal cues, such as hand movements, facial expressions, and eye contact, which may reveal hidden emotional reactions; verify and don't make assumptions about what is happening.
- Make a conscious effort to identify and consider each other's situation and point of view.
- Demonstrate deep caring and kindness toward each other's well-being.

Perseverance
- Strive to understand each other's thoughts, feelings, and perspectives by asking questions and listening until the conversation or consultation comes to a natural ending.
- Share and consult about our thoughts, feelings, and perspectives with each other openly and regularly to gain and maintain mutual understanding.
- Focus on the overall goal or core values we wish to achieve in a consultation, even when disagreements arise, and strive to achieve a unified outcome.

Reflection

- Listen carefully to each other and consider the words and feelings that are shared.
- Pause to seek inspiration and think carefully before sharing thoughts and feelings.
- Search for information to clarify our thinking, analyze our options, and conduct thorough consultations.

Learning Activities:

1. Choose an issue that's causing us some challenges and take turns sharing and discussing it back and forth, with the listener summarizing periodically to check for understanding. The goal is to apply Compassion to understand each other's views, not necessarily to solve the current issue. If speaking to each other is causing us difficulties, we can sometimes try writing down our thoughts and sharing them that way, going back and forth as needed.

2. Identify the specific positive and negative feelings that could arise in each of the situations listed below:

   a. There has been an injustice in our neighborhood, workplace, or the country where we live
   b. We go out on a date to a concert for our anniversary
   c. We have been asked to carry out a specific act of community service
   d. One of us burns and ruins a special dinner
   e. One of us participates in a spiritual practice, and the other doesn't
   f. We take our first vacation in five years
   g. We unexpectedly receive a large sum of money
   h. We become parents (or grandparents)

3. To expand our skill in identifying feelings, think about two different scenarios from our life, and then practice using these phrases a few times: "When I see or hear ____ (or when ____ happens), I feel ____."

4. Create a "love map" (Idea Source: John M. Gottman and Nan Silver): It's important and potentially unifying for couples to know one another well through observing, sharing, and listening. The goal of this activity is to map out our partner's life as we know it now. Then, we will fill in the gaps together, without negatively commenting on what the other was unaware of.

   Each of us begins with our own piece of paper and some writing or drawing utensils, and we will do the first part of the activity individually. On the paper, we will use Creativity to describe our partner in words and drawings in whatever way works for us. We could draw a tree, squares, circles, pictures, or anything else that displays our partner's life, and then add words to it. Here are some examples of topics, in no particular order, but we can go beyond these as needed:

   - Virtues they exhibit and love
   - Feelings they express most easily
   - Feelings most difficult to acknowledge and express
   - Emotional and spiritual wounds still healing
   - Preferred type of work; professional aspirations
   - Favorite activities, service choices, and high priorities for spending time
   - Closest friends
   - Current or recurring fears, stresses, sadnesses, and worries
   - Common irritants

- Purpose(s) in life
- Views about children, parenting, and grandparenting
- Philosophies/practices of parenting
- Life dreams
- Religious/spiritual beliefs and activities
- Basic philosophy of life
- Favorite music, games, movies, TV shows, podcasts...
- What like to read
- Most special times in life
- Childhood traumas/stresses
- Major aspirations and hopes
- Likely actions on receiving a major sum of money
- What they do to recharge energy; to relax
- Favorite hobbies; attitudes about hobbies
- Dream vacation spot(s)
- Preferred ways to celebrate (include if likes or doesn't like surprises)
- Where turns for help and support
- Preferred ways to exercise
- Important events coming up and feelings related to them
- Medical concerns
- Concerns about family members

Example: One person could draw a circle for "Current fears, stresses, and worries", and then list in the circle about their partner they are concerned about: "Adjusting to their new job and their parents' health". The partner could draw a circle for the other showing their "Most special times in life" and then write in the circle: "The couple vacation we took last year" and "Tutoring a teen to succeed in school".

Reflect and Consult: Once we have both completed our maps, share them, discuss them, and add to them. We can consider such questions as these:

- What were the surprises?
- What did we appreciate learning?
- Were we able to share and learn without becoming upset that our partner was unaware of something significant about us?
- Do we feel confident we know one another better? That we know one another well?

Related Activity: Now draw a map together of our couple relationship. Consider using Reflection and consultation to respond to these questions:

a. What are our goals as a couple?
b. What activities do we do together?
c. What do we do individually with agreement from our partner, and how do these activities enrich us and our relationship?
d. What roles and responsibilities do we carry out as parents or grandparents?
e. What are the primary relationships we have with family members? How healthy are these relationships?
f. What significant concerns are on our minds and hearts?
g. What are the joys we feel?

Couple Reflection and Consultation:

Throughout this couple guide, there are invitations to practice the virtue of Reflection about your interactions and connection. This practice gives you opportunities to celebrate progress and consult to address issues.

1. How can we increase our ability to identify and express feelings?
2. What feelings are most difficult for us to admit we are experiencing?
3. When do we need time alone to reflect before sharing what is on our minds or hearts?
4. When is it especially important that we understand with our hearts as well as our minds?
5. When is it unwise for us to express our feelings immediately to each other?
6. What feelings do we especially want to know about when our partner is experiencing them?
7. What actions and environment help us experience safety when we are vulnerable with each other and expressing our feelings?
8. What are some ways we can stay current with each other's life? What frequency is needed?
9. How does having a deep understanding of each other contribute to our friendship and relationship?
10. What would demonstrate to us that we are skilled with emotional intelligence and emotionally intimate as a couple?

Unifier 6: Respecting Each Other

*"Each of us has 100 percent responsibility
to create our connection
because we are each whole beings."*
Kathlyn Hendricks and Gay Hendricks

Focus Statement: We show Respect to each other as equal partners in our relationship, share decision-making, and appreciate each other's contributions toward our well-being in all aspects of our lives.

Deeper Learning:

When we function in partnership, we demonstrate Respect for each other's abilities and efforts. We create a balance, treating one another equally as worthy and noble human beings. We value one another's body, mind, heart, and soul. We show Respect for one another's virtue strengths, talents, and skills. We appreciate and champion each other's education and career accomplishments. We are grateful for each other's actions supporting our home and family. We strive to understand, value, and practice our cultural heritage(s) in ways that contribute to unity. We listen to and celebrate each other's accomplishments. We function together as a team.

We use Justice in our relationship, which empowers us to treat each other fairly. We strive to eliminate patterns of unequal power, domination, aggression, and control over each other. We address areas where we need personal growth and in any areas where we discover imbalances.

As we strive to create an equal and respectful partnership that contributes to couple unity, we consult about our roles and responsibilities and how we can offer Service to each other to maintain well-being. We learn what assists each other to be successful in achieving goals and dreams, and we do our best to be supportive. [See "Unifier 13: Giving Thoughtful Service".] We consider this:

> "In couple relationships ... the well-being of each partner is supported equally, both in the short and long term."[30] "Marital Equality"

We reflect on and consult about our experiences to determine which tasks or roles are best suited for each of us and how we can support one another. What we do may differ for each of us, yet we remain equal partners.

We seek out learning opportunities to expand our capabilities and contribute more effectively. We assess the models we learned from growing up or that operate in our friends' or families' lives, and we are conscious about what we imitate or eliminate. We examine our expectations of what each other does and how actions are carried out to ensure we are not imposing unreasonable standards on each other. We consider fairness as we engage in various activities and create and manage our home environment and household tasks.

Sharing from Experience: *"It's both fun and funny to look back on our early years and realize just how much we have both changed as our relationship has matured. We are far from the days when either of us was concerned with spending a few dollars without consulting the other person, just as we are far from the days when we felt that we both needed to be active and equal participants in every aspect of everything. Today, we are both deeply invested in raising our children, cooking, cleaning, developing and managing the budget, and so forth, but we no longer attempt to be equal in the tasks themselves.*

For us, we are equal at the strategic level and allow for differences at the tactical level.

"When new issues crop up or we need to support the regular maintenance of our big decisions (examples: parenting approaches, budget development…), we are both equally and actively engaged. But for day-to-day implementation, we each have our strengths or otherwise have areas that are just logistically more straightforward for one person to address than the other.

"On those infrequent occasions when we can enjoy a 'day in the life' of our partner, it's much easier to appreciate the many things that the other person does that we would not otherwise even think to notice. If both parties are striving to contribute to the whole to the best of their ability, then the breakdown of specific tasks will fall out where it's most appropriate. This delineation is generally along the lines of each partner's preferences and skills."

Our equality and practice of Respect influence how we make decisions and who initiates actions. When we communicate, our tone of voice, the words we use, and our body language all convey Respect. [See "Core Element B: Reflection and Consultation".]

We rely on each other for advice and wisdom. We build mutual understanding, determine our desired outcomes, and carry out actions together. We share our dreams and consult about our goals. We are fair and thoughtful and not self-centered:

"It took us a long time to realize that relationships only exist between equals. Each of us has 100 percent responsibility to create our connection because we are each whole beings. People get into trouble when they stop acting from full creative participation. If you take less than

100 percent responsibility, it's easy to feel that other people are at fault. ... [T]rue responsibility is not about finding fault or accepting blame. It is about a genuine insight into the causes of an action or event. ... When true responsibility is taken, learning can take place."[31]
Kathlyn Hendricks and Gay Hendricks

With equality as a foundational principle, we can function as loving friends and partners. This physical, mental, emotional, and spiritual partnership is vital for us to create a happy and lasting, unity-filled relationship. Behaving with equality also provides a healthy model for our children, families, and community. We are true companions to each other.

Examples:

- Consult about the roles we each fulfill within the home and family, and adjust them as needed to create greater fairness.
- Consult on work choices outside the home or in a home office to determine whether we are meeting our needs and whether our structure is respectful and fair.
- Identify a talent or ability in each of us and express appreciation or encouragement to develop it further.

Applying Virtues:

Below are some practical ways to incorporate virtues into daily practices with the theme of this chapter.

Justice
- Evaluate the fairness of our current roles and responsibilities and adjust as necessary.

- Request consultation courageously when we suspect unequal or disrespectful actions may be occurring.
- Challenge each other and consult when something happens that appears to have bias, prejudice, or unexamined assumptions about roles.

Respect
- Demonstrate confidence in each person's voice as a vital contribution to a mutual decision.
- Value each other as truly equal human beings and communicate and act in ways that demonstrate this.
- See each other as functioning in a balanced and equal partnership, even when in different roles or carrying out different responsibilities.

Trust
- Count on each other to carry out our agreed-upon actions without controlling or micromanaging each other.
- Demonstrate confidence in each other's abilities and judgment through deferring and delegating as appropriate.
- Share honestly with each other the thoughts and motivations related to topics and plans under consultation.

Learning Activities:

1. Identify an area of our couple interactions where we are usually consistent at practicing equality and fairness, and express appreciation to each other.

2. Choose and collaborate on one or two projects. Consider the strength of our relationship, physical well-being, and emotional states to discern whether an activity will likely

be constructive and skill-building or cause conflict or other problems. Below are some ideas.

- Arranging books on a bookshelf
- Gardening
- A camping trip/travel in nature
- Rearranging or decorating a room
- Readying a vehicle and packing for a trip
- Building something for the home
- Putting a puzzle together
- Taking care of a friend's child
- Cooking a meal
- Cleaning out and organizing a cupboard, drawer, or closet

Reflect and Consult [Suggestion: Read all the questions to begin with and then initiate consultation about the whole activity]:

a. How well did we complete the tasks?
b. How effectively did we cooperate and assist one another?
c. Were either of us overly helpful to the other? What was the response?
d. How did we handle differences of opinion?
e. Did we need to involve others in support? Were we in agreement about their involvement and roles?
f. Were we able to listen carefully, demonstrate Respect for each other's input and actions, complete the tasks successfully, and end the project in unity?
g. Did we consult about anything from our lives during the project that we might not have talked about as easily in another circumstance?

3. Examine our furniture and decorations and consider how they contribute to our lives and demonstrate our Respect for ourselves, our beliefs, and our cultural heritage(s). Consult about and decide on any changes we will make.

4. Identify a talent or skill that one of us has that we have not been utilizing or appreciating, and begin to use it or show appreciation for it.

5. Consider the couples we have known in the past, currently in our lives, or observed in books, movies, or other media. What are some ways they demonstrate equality and fairness between them? What examples do we want to follow?

6. Identify and consult about an area where we have not been practicing equality and fairness as much as we would like. Create a concrete plan to address the issues we have identified.

Couple Reflection and Consultation:

Throughout this couple guide, there are invitations to practice the virtue of Reflection about your interactions and connection. This practice gives you opportunities to celebrate progress and consult to address issues.

1. What are our beliefs about equality between partners? About how to demonstrate Respect between partners? Are we open to incorporating these concepts into our life as a couple? Why or why not?

2. What are some of our experiences of practicing partnership, companionship, and equality in our life together?

3. How do the virtues of Justice and Respect affect or encourage unity between us?
4. What different roles do we each have? How do these affect our perception of equality happening in our relationship?
5. What can ensure that our behaviors within our relationship and family demonstrate fairness and equality?
6. How do our incomes affect the balance of equality we experience?
7. What skills are we willing to learn that would enhance our ability to expand beyond what might be considered traditional roles and responsibilities? How will we learn and apply them?

Unifier 7: Loving One Another

"I am convinced that keeping the emotional love tank full
is as important to a marriage as
maintaining the proper oil level is to an automobile."
Gary Chapman

Focus Statement: We ensure we have loving thoughts about each other and express loving words and actions to one another to sustain our mutual loving feelings.

Deeper Learning:

Throughout our relationship, feelings of love have attracted us to one another. We feel love on many levels, physically, emotionally, mentally, and spiritually. As our relationship develops and we make efforts to connect on all these levels, our love evolves into a deeper, more fulfilling experience. We don't try to make distinctions between being "in love", "cherishing", and "loving each other"—these are all aspects of a growing and expanding love that unifies us.

Expressing Love

As we strengthen our ability to think loving thoughts, share loving words, and carry out loving actions, the quality of love between us strengthens. Love is a vital element in our emotional support for one another and in forming a close bond of unity, both of which are essential to a thriving relationship. Our Trust and Compassion create a safe environment to express our feelings of love. We can be vulnerable and intimate.

Some people use the word "cherish" when describing how they love their partner:

> "When we cherish our partner, we feel that they're irreplaceable. We simply cannot imagine our lives without them, even when times are rough. We find ways to tell them that we appreciate them, and do that often. This builds trust in the relationship. Cherishing and commitment go together, but they're different. Commitment is really a verb because it is the actions we take daily to let our partner know we are with them, and that we make decisions with them in mind."[32]
> Mary Beth George

As we experience each other's loving words and actions, we grow in our understanding of what communicates love to each of us. We may have different preferences. Dr. Gary Chapman has written books about five love languages with the theme that our partner's chosen method of expressing love to us affects our ability to perceive and internalize it as an expression of love. He says:

> "I am convinced that keeping the emotional love tank full is as important to a marriage as maintaining the proper oil level is to an automobile. Running your marriage on an empty 'love tank' may cost you even more than trying to drive your car without oil."[33] Gary Chapman

Below is a summary of the Five Love Languages from Chapman's work, with examples of how to practice them:

1. **"Words of Affirmation:** verbal compliments; words of appreciation, praise, and encouragement; kind words;

expressions of appreciation for the other's positive qualities and actions.

2. "**Gifts:** tangible objects freely offered; gifts of any size, shape, color, or price; gifts that indicate thoughtfulness; visual symbols of love with no strings attached and no attempt to cover up a failure or apologize; unexpected gifts, not just on special occasions.

3. "**Acts of Service:** things done willingly for the other; offers of helpfulness; timely and positive response to requests (not demands) of the other; acts of kindness; favors done with a loving attitude (not fear, guilt, or resentment); acts that demonstrate equality and partnership.

4. "**Quality Time:** being available; doing something enjoyable and interactive together; giving uninterrupted, undivided, and focused attention; participating in quality conversations in which both talk and listen; creating memorable moments; intimate revealing of self.

5. "**Physical Touch:** loving (never abusive) physical contact at appropriate times and places; tender hugs, touches, or pats on the arm, shoulder, or back; back or foot rubs or massages; kissing; holding hands; holding while comforting; intimate touch and sex."[34] Summarized from Gary Chapman

Matching our expressions of love with what each other most wants and needs to receive can establish or restore our unity. We want to meet one another's emotional needs, but we recognize that we have knowledge and skills to acquire to be as effective as we would like to be. [There's an activity later in this chapter so you can better understand and practice these concepts.]

Sharing from Experience: *"We kept going round and round with complaints about each other. We were both frustrated and unhappy. One of us felt criticized most of the time. There were no positive words. The other kept feeling lonely and emotionally abandoned. Reading 'The Five Love Languages' saved our relationship.*

"It took practicing Perseverance for us to go in a better direction, but the answer was quite simple. One of us needed to receive the Love Language of hearing many positive 'words of affirmation' to feel loved. Any critical words then had twice the negative impact. The other one of us needed the Love Language of 'quality time' that included undivided attention and time together. We looked at our schedules and commitments and made some important changes to make that time happen. We are much happier today with both of us giving each other the preferred Love Language."

Here is more about nurturing love as a couple:

"You cannot make yourself feel love or make another person love you, just as you cannot create your own heartbeat. Loving feelings grow and flourish naturally in the presence of certain conditions, in the presence of loving behavior. To behave in a way that nurtures love, you must feel worthy of giving and receiving love. ...

"It is not unusual for loving feelings to be covered over by hurt, anger, resentment, or fear. At such times, love feels dead or absent. Conflicts are the result of natural differences between partners, but most people do not know how to handle conflicts well. Painful emotions or deadness to love is a sign of partners handling conflicts poorly. Hurt, anger, resentment, or fear can last for years if not dealt with. When you feel other intense emotions, you will not feel love at the same time. The unpleasant emotion must be attended to properly so that healing occurs, which allows the flow of loving feelings again. Most often, love only feels dead, but is waiting, ready to come to life with the hope that conflicts can be resolved. ...

"A happy marriage needs a mixture of intimate feelings and loving commitment. Loving commitment is determination and resolve that the loved person should flourish."[35] Sandra Gray Bender

There are times when we fall into the habit of assuming we love each other and fail to express it explicitly. We might think, "My partner knows that I love them. Otherwise, I would not have chosen them, and I would not have stayed with them." It can be beneficial to reassure each other that we love and care for one another, especially when discussing difficult issues.

In times of difficulty, old messages from our pasts when we felt unloved or abandoned emotionally or physically can prompt us to feel insecure. An expression of love at that time brings us back into the present, builds security, and demonstrates our Trust. Additionally, when we regularly express loving feelings, they flourish and contribute to our sense of harmony in our relationship.

Note: For more information on understanding and expressing feelings, refer to "Unifier 5: Understanding Each Other".

Emotional Interdependence

As individuals, we must balance being emotionally connected and interdependent, along with being somewhat independent. We must be mature enough to function effectively on our own, if necessary, but we also choose to be partnered and work together as a healthy unit. As with the two wings of a bird, both of us are unique, with neither the left nor the right one the same; yet, both are essential for flight, and ideally, both are similar in strength.

As we learn how to live with each other as loving partners, we draw on each other's unique strengths. If one of us is often emotionally weak, needy, or overly dependent, we cannot "fly" effectively. If one of us tends to be overly strong and dominant, again, the "flying pattern" is uneven, or "flying" fails altogether. It benefits us to:

- Engage in personal growth
- Have honest and ongoing communications
- Turn to each other to meet our primary emotional needs
- Do our best to demonstrate equality in our actions and attitudes

In "Becoming Your True Self", we found this view about the importance of achieving this balance between us:

"The loving capacity includes not only the ability to love but also the ability to be loved—to attract love. We cannot have lovers without loved ones. If we do not know how to be loved or cannot accept it, then we frustrate others who are struggling to develop their capacity to love. Not accepting someone's love is very frequently experienced as rejection and does untold amounts of damage...."[36]
Daniel C. Jordan

When we consider the love we share as true partners, we also consider other important factors that unite us: our equality, intimacy, fidelity, sexual relations, childbearing, and childrearing. These are integrated and interconnected strengths.

Note: If it seems to you that emotional dependence and interdependence are areas with a lot of imbalances or struggles, it may be wise for you to seek assistance from a professional.

Connections Between Personality and Love

To truly show Respect and love for one another, we must first understand who we are. This means recognizing our unique personality—the distinct patterns of thoughts, feelings, and behaviors that shape how we interact with the world.

Personality influences nearly every aspect of our lives:

- How we communicate and connect with people: Are we expressive or reserved? Do we prefer deep conversations or lighthearted exchanges?
- How we organize our time, spaces, and tasks: Are we structured and methodical, or do we thrive on spontaneity?
- How we handle feedback and criticism: Do we receive it openly or struggle with defensiveness?
- How we regulate our emotions: Are we naturally steady, or do we experience emotions intensely?
- And so much more

Virtues shape how we navigate these traits in a way that fosters love and harmony. For instance, a highly organized person can develop Flexibility to accommodate a more spontaneous partner. Likewise, someone who struggles with criticism can cultivate Humility to avoid defensiveness and seek a deeper understanding of how to grow with their partner.

As relationship experts Les and Leslie Parrott, along with David H. Olson, put it:

"Our personalities play a central role in our love lives. Personality traits, for example, shape how we communicate and how we like someone to communicate with us. Personality shapes how we give and receive affection, whether we tend to show up early or late, and whether we like routine or variety."[37]

Personality and Character: What's the Difference?

While personality is an inherent part of who we are, often noticeable even from childhood, character virtues are qualities we cultivate over time. Our personalities might evolve slightly, but our virtues are something we can actively work on and strengthen daily and throughout our lives.

Interestingly, our personalities can influence the virtues we develop more easily. For instance, a naturally extroverted person may find it easier to express Politeness and Sociability, while an introvert might need to be more intentional about it. However, that doesn't mean an introvert is any less capable of demonstrating this virtue. In fact, because they deeply value meaningful interactions, introverts may cultivate Politeness and Sociability in a more thoughtful and impactful way that fosters strong, lasting connections with a close-knit group. By recognizing it as an area for growth, an introvert can develop this virtue with purpose, often bringing a level of depth and sincerity that makes their interactions even more enriching.

Embracing Each Other's Uniqueness

Understanding each other's personality traits prompts us to appreciate one another more deeply. Instead of letting differences create distance, we can use them to strengthen our relationships.

For example, one of us is an introvert who needs solitude to recharge, while the other is an extrovert who thrives on social interaction. By practicing Moderation and Flexibility, we can find a balance that ensures our individual needs are met while nurturing our bond.

When we recognize and honor each other's personalities, we create a relationship built on mutual respect, understanding, and love. By strengthening our virtues, we enhance the way our personalities shine, which makes our connections even more fulfilling.

[See "Core Element C: Virtues Growth" for information on loving each other's virtues.]

Examples:

- Express love in the other's favorite way of receiving it.
- Share something that we love about each other.
- Choose and give a card that expresses our loving feelings.
- Do something that contributes to each other's well-being in a way that uniquely comes from each of our personalities.

Applying Virtues:

Below are some practical ways to incorporate virtues into daily practices with the theme of this chapter.

Compassion
- Ensure we understand and help meet each other's needs, even when our perspectives or ways of thinking about the matter are different.
- Strive to see each other's perspectives, understand each other's feelings, and consider each other's well-being in our responses.
- Create a loving and caring time for each of us to share and listen to our feelings, potentially during a consultation about a topic.

Positive Spirit
- Focus our thoughts and attention on what we love about each other, rather than dwelling on each other's faults.
- Express loving feelings in words and actions daily or as often as possible.
- Respond with joy to each other's expressions of love.

Service
- Assist each other to understand and manage emotions, such as love, and express them effectively, beneficially, and consistently.
- Show consistent loving words, actions, and support to each other.
- Seek expert knowledge or professional assistance as needed for us to achieve a high-quality relationship.

Learning Activities:

1. Visit the https://www.5lovelanguages.com website. Use the provided assessment to learn how we prefer to receive expressions of love. It's usually helpful to identify a primary and a secondary Love Language. [An alternative is to obtain one of the Five Love Languages books by Gary Chapman.] Consult about a few simple ways to improve our expressions of love and start implementing them. Reflect on and consult about what is working well and where a change in direction is needed, without becoming critical of what hasn't happened in the past. While engaging with all of the Five Love Languages can benefit us, we strive for consistency with at least each other's primary Love Language.

2. What are five aspects of each other's personality that we appreciate? Consult about a new way that one of our personality traits can benefit the other or other people. What is one aspect of each other's personality that sometimes challenges us? What virtues or approaches would lead us to accept and adjust to these more difficult traits? Apply these for an agreed period and then reflect on the outcome.

3. Do a new and challenging activity together. Share three virtues we noticed and appreciated in each other during the activity.

Couple Reflection and Consultation:

Throughout this couple guide, there are invitations to practice the virtue of Reflection about your interactions and connection. This practice gives you opportunities to celebrate progress and consult to address issues.

1. What are our favorite ways to express love to one another? Are these received positively? Why or why not?
2. What are our primary and secondary "Love Languages"? What are some of the best actions we can take to meet each other's need for feeling loved?
3. What mutual way could we express love at the same time?
4. What negative feelings are interfering with feeling loving? How can these be addressed and resolved? [See "Unifier 17: Resolving and Rebounding".]
5. When do we feel the happiest? What makes it easier for these times to happen?
6. What do we perceive as some of the similarities between character virtues and personality traits?
7. What do we perceive as some of the differences between character virtues and personality traits?
8. What are some personality traits we each have that we could draw on to enliven our life together?
9. What are some of the virtues we admire in each other? How can we express gratitude or praise for these virtues?
10. What virtues would we like to see more of in our relationship?

Unifier 8: Appreciating One Another

*"... [A] person needs to ramp up the positives
so the good-to-bad ratio doesn't fall to a risky level.
Couples in solid, lasting relationships do this naturally."*
Tara Parker-Pope

Focus Statement: We use positive words of appreciation to acknowledge the helpful contributions and thoughtful actions we each bring to our relationship, family, and home.

Deeper Learning:

Our sincere and loving words have tremendous power to influence and encourage one another. They focus us positively on what we each contribute and lead us to stop magnifying each other's faults. Encouraging words can inspire us to move in positive directions and apply Creativity and Service to achieve goals, try new activities, and much more. When we feel self-doubt, encouragement gives us the courage and confidence to move forward. Encouragement enhances our peaceful interactions and deepens our passion for what's important to us.

We may automatically look for what doesn't go well rather than what does. It's often easier to criticize than to see and appreciate what each of us does well. However, we must have multiple positive interactions with each other for every negative one:

"In real life, no couple can keep a running tally of positive and negative displays. There are hundreds of them that happen in any given day. But in a practical sense, the lesson is that a single 'I'm sorry' after bad behavior isn't enough. For every snide comment or negative outburst..., a person needs to ramp up the positives so the good-to-bad ratio doesn't fall to a risky level. Couples in solid, lasting relationships do this naturally. Sometimes the positives are spoken. 'You look nice today, honey.' 'That color looks good on you.' 'What a great meal.' 'You're a good dad.' Sometimes the positives are gestures—pats on the hand or back, a hug, a tousle of the hair, a kiss for no reason."[38] Tara Parker-Pope

Positive and constructive words increase our Respect for each other and build our self-Respect, one of the keys to happiness. These types of words lovingly soften our hearts and prompt us to do our best with our actions.

Using Virtue Language™ as a specific skill to affirm virtues in each other fosters love, appreciation, and happiness between us. This outcome is especially likely when we are sincere and include specifics about the actions each other did. Here are some simple examples:

- "Thank you for your Flexibility in changing your appointment when I needed you to take me to work."
- "I admire your Perseverance! You had to ask your manager for a pay increase several times before they agreed."
- "I love how you show Compassion when your friends need help!"

It takes practice to look consciously for each other's positive actions and speak specifically about them, and it's worth the effort and very affirming for both of us. Having someone notice our use of a virtue encourages us to continue behaving in a positive manner. Using virtue words recognizes the gems of each other's heart and soul.

Someone Shares Their Experience: *"I'm sick with a cold and have been sneezing and coughing. Everywhere I turn, there's a tissue box waiting for me to cover a sneeze, cough, or drippy nose. I'm REALLY grateful to my partner for all these tissue boxes; they made me wonderful soup, too. I have repeatedly thanked them for their Compassion and Service in taking care of me so well."*

We have also learned that if we follow a positive statement with "but" and then express a complaint or criticism, we eliminate any positive effect from the initial statement. The negative comment also seems to cause more hurt when it follows a positive statement.

Often, it's beneficial for us to consult and determine how we can apply virtues such as Compassion, Justice, or Creativity to a situation. Then we can observe how applying them improves it. We also do our best to acknowledge others for their positive behaviors throughout the resolution of the problem.

Sharing from Experience: *"I believe it's especially important to look for opportunities for appreciation during times of difficulties. We recently went through a period with many things going wrong with our home, work, and vehicles. We had to apply Creativity to come up with solutions and then use Purposefulness and Perseverance in carrying them out. Friends and family helped us through all of it, and we saw their faces light up when we shared with them the virtues we saw them use to help us. We are grateful to them for accompanying us so well."*

Appreciating each other shows we are grateful for who each other is as a person and the contributions each of us makes to our relationship, home, and family. When we express appreciation, we affirm the virtue of Excellence, even when one of us performs a task or role, as these positive words provide encouragement and loving support. Gratitude benefits our relationship and generates joy:

> "At home the only currency exchange is how you and your mate express your feelings about each other, and gratitude is an often-overlooked commodity. It's easier to say 'Thanks' when you're feeling good about your marriage. It's harder when you're dissatisfied. But gratitude, and its expression, is not just a reflection of a happy marriage; it is one of the causes."[39] Paul Coleman

Sharing from Experience: *"I had a very difficult first marriage. Now that I'm in a better situation with a new partner, I never want to take them and everything they do for us for granted. I'm thankful for even the little things. If they hand me a towel, cook a good meal, buy household supplies, consult with me about my work, and so on, I say, 'Thank you'. They tell me how appreciated they feel, and we are both happy to participate fully in our relationship."*

As we reflect on our lives and behavior, we can be grateful for the growth we've experienced. Perhaps we were able to apply Flexibility when a friend wanted to make different plans. Maybe our child had a difficult day, and we applied Compassion through listening well and offering sincere encouragement. We discovered we were able to apply Politeness and Sociability with a difficult relative and neighbor. When we see each other's successes in these types of circumstances, we can celebrate and appreciate each other's progress.

Gratitude and thankfulness are similar:

"Without thankfulness people would stay focused on negativity. They would do nothing but whine and complain. They would miss the beauty of life and the power of learning, especially during difficult times. ... No matter how difficult or dark things become, there is always light. There is something to learn in every painful situation. In fact, sometimes when you look back at a really hard test in your life and realize what you learned, that is when you feel the most grateful of all."[40] Linda Kavelin Popov

Examples:

- "Thank you for using Creativity to cook a great meal."
- "I'm grateful for your Dependability in managing our finances."
- "I appreciate your Purposefulness in planning educational activities for our children."
- "I love how we applied our Unity when we painted and decorated our home together."
- "You're such a great neighbor!" The ways you demonstrate Respect toward us bring us happiness."

Applying Virtues:

Below are some practical ways to incorporate virtues into daily practices with the theme of this chapter.

Justice
- Observe and acknowledge each other's positive actions.
- Note the facts about all the good that we do and share them with each other, friends, and family members

- Appreciate each other for the responsibilities we carry out consistently

Positive Spirit
- Show enthusiasm and appreciation for each other's contributions to our relationship, home, and family.
- Celebrate anniversaries, each other's accomplishments, and when we achieve significant relationship milestones.
- Experience and express gratitude to one another for the unity between us.

Truthfulness
- Recognize and honestly acknowledge the abilities, gifts, and talents each of us brings to our relationship.
- Use sincere words to share both the positive and the challenging aspects as we strive for our well-being and unity as a couple.
- Acknowledge the virtue strengths each other applies to our lives.

Learning Activities:

1. Take turns practicing the skill of Virtue Language and acknowledge each other for something we each did recently. Reflect together on how it feels to receive such positive words from each other. Begin with one acknowledgment a day and then strive to increase the frequency until it feels natural and becomes part of the culture of our relationship.

2. Each day for a week, share three things we are grateful for in our life and home. Continue this practice if it's positive and effective. Invite people we know to participate in this practice as well.

Couple Reflection and Consultation:

Throughout this couple guide, there are invitations to practice the virtue of Reflection about your interactions and connection. This practice gives you opportunities to celebrate progress and consult to address issues.

1. How does it feel when we encourage each other? How do we respond?
2. How does it feel when we show appreciation or gratitude to each other? How do we respond?
3. Do we respond differently if we receive appreciation for tasks that we view as routine parts of our role, whether with each other or at home? Why?
4. How does our partner feel if we discount the appreciation one of us gives?
5. When we have more positive interactions than negative ones, how does it affect our relationship? Our well-being?
6. Are there any recent accomplishments that we want to celebrate? How will we do this?
7. What are we grateful for in our relationship? Our family? Our home? Our friends? Our community?

Unifier 9: Harmonizing Our Communications

"When two people are communicating heart-to-heart,
they always feel more respect and caring afterward
than before they spoke."
Richard Carlson and Joseph Bailey

Focus Statement: We stay thoughtfully aware of each other's well-being, striving to demonstrate Compassion, Respect, and Self-Discipline before, during, and after our communications.

Deeper Learning:

We are happy with our interactions at times, and at other times, not so much. Our skillfulness affects the quality of our lives and contributes to our having a thriving relationship. Our stress levels spike upward when our words lead to disunity and pain. However, when our communications grow unity and understanding, our stress levels are lower, and we feel more connected and happier.

It's often a challenge for us—and every human being—to communicate smoothly. We gained our experience with communication from our families, friends, and teachers while growing up, as well as through the culture around us and our relationship experiences. We have brought all this learning into our relationship. Sometimes, we learned positive skills, and sometimes, we learned poor habits!

Communication is a broad topic, and we read materials, watch videos, and access other helpful resources to improve. In this Unifier, we focus on how to prevent some of the ways we can get into difficulty, and we share some of the positive skills we have discovered.

Caring for Our Well-Being

Important or sensitive communications tend to happen better when we reflect ahead of time on what we will say, how we will deliver it, and when we will raise the topic. We can assess the timing or content of what we want to say to see if it would cause harm instead of creating benefit.

We learned through experience that it's wise to address our own and each other's physical, mental, emotional, and spiritual well-being before communicating. This prevents our words and tone of voice from being unnecessarily negative. We request time to take care of our needs or make suggestions to each other.

We use the tool called H.A.L.T., as it prompts us to apply Compassion, Respect, and Self-Discipline. We can stop or postpone (halt) our communication and address our needs as much as possible, such as these:

- **H:** Are we **H**ungry? – Have something to eat
- **A:** Are we **A**ngry? – Take time to calm down and re-center
- **L:** Do we have **L**ow Energy? – Recharge with time alone or time with others
- **T:** Are we **T**ired? – Take a rest break or sleep

We also discovered that taking a H.A.L.T. break during a consultation benefits us if we begin escalating into discord. During the pause break, we take time for Reflection and assess:

- Are our feelings hurt, and why?
- Are we either dominating our partner or not sharing important thoughts and feelings?

- Is our ego in the mode of wanting to be "right" about something and insisting on that, rather than striving for unity?

When we come back together, we may choose to be vulnerable and share what came from our Reflection time. We then create space for true consultation where we learn, understand, and work together to achieve a unified outcome.

Sharing from Experience: *"We use H.A.L.T. as one way to proactively avoid conflict. However, we have noticed that when we use it regularly, it can indicate a systemic issue that we need to address. For example, we noticed that one of us was so constantly tired from a long daily work commute that there was regularly no energy to connect or consult. Issues were postponed so much that resentment and conflict began to become common. It could not continue that way.*

"We organized our lives and children so that we had a few hours to reflect and consult about the postponed issues and what could improve our patterns. We considered all the options and concerns, and ultimately we decided to move closer to the work location. It was a major upheaval and change, but the quality of our relationship and family life has significantly improved."

We may encounter difficulties by proceeding with a consultation when a pause, break, or even sleeping overnight would be more beneficial. Pausing can be kind, merciful, and gentle with one another. We pause when we notice we are no longer listening and participating effectively, or when either or both of us are getting angry or stressed. Letting the feelings calm and subside for 15-20 minutes makes it easier for us to begin consulting again.

If taking a break results in one of us leaving our home, we try to practice Respect and let the other partner know where we are going and how long we will likely be gone. It's also wise for us to agree on which of us will reinitiate consultation and when, and then do so without reminding.

We have various ways we calm our feelings. Physical activity can be a good approach—individually or together—such as exercising, chopping wood, or cleaning. Alternatively, we try playing music, meditating, listening to a positive podcast, watching an uplifting video, spending time in nature, writing in a journal, or praying.

We reflect during the break or when we resume, using questions such as these:

- What feelings and thoughts arose within me that led to my negative behavior?
- Were they rooted in my resistance, judgments, or fears?
- Was my ego involved? Did it get bruised by something?
- How might I have handled my feelings more skillfully?
- Would it have been possible to see what was going on as it was happening, and show Compassion for both of us at that time?
- Are there actions that I or we can do now to make this type of behavior or reaction less likely to happen in the future?
- Are there warning signs or remedies that I or we can identify to prevent future issues? Is there a way we can lighten up our interactions effectively, such as by using humor?
- Is there a quotation, prayer, or simple self-talk that I could use to defuse a situation or manage my feelings as soon as they begin to escalate? For example: "Okay, it's time for me to breathe deeply and to calm down now."

Being Kind and Respectful

When we are thoughtful, gentle, and kind as we begin communicating with one another, we are more likely to maintain a unified connection between us. A constructive consultation is unlikely to happen if we start with an attack and use harsh and critical words. As our communication progresses, we need to apply tact along with our Truthfulness. We may be frustrated or even angry about an issue we are consulting about, and our thoughts and feelings are important to share. What is essential, however, is always caring about our unity and the integrity of the bond between us.

As we consistently speak from our hearts and practice Respect, our communications will become increasingly harmonious. Here is a goal to aim for:

"Communication that comes from the heart has the ability to transform. Heart-to-heart communication helps us get past our separate realities to the common ground of mental health. It helps our thinking evolve and helps us see issues in a different perspective. When two people communicate heart-to-heart, they feel more respect and caring afterward than before they spoke."[41] Richard Carlson and Joseph Bailey

As we talked about in "Core Element C: Virtues Growth", here again, is this reminder:

"You will always have some complaints about the person you live with. But there's a world of difference between complaint and criticism. A complaint focuses on a specific behavior or event. ... In contrast, a criticism is global and expresses negative feelings or opinions about the other's character or personality.... Statements that contain complaints are soft start-ups, while those that criticize are harsh start-ups."[42] John M. Gottman and Nan Silver

Sharing from Experience: *"We are gaining a deeper understanding of how we respond to situations and the ways we communicate. Often, we realize we are unskillful because we learned from watching parents argue a lot. These insights are helping us make conscious choices to respond better. We occasionally spot times when we can lighten up and laugh, which diffuses tension. We have also begun to realize that focusing on negatives doesn't always improve the situation. In other words, being aware of communications we don't like doesn't seem to be as helpful as time spent talking about what would be better and how to achieve it."*

Effective Dialogue

We began to learn about sharing and listening in "Unifier 5: Understanding Each Other". Now, we are going deeper into strengthening our skills:

"In the case of dialogue, with conscious effort we can choose to stay with the experience our partner is describing—even though it may feel like a blow to us—without becoming defensive, even if the events being described contradict our memory of them. This does not mean that we agree with what our partner says or how she or he remembers events. Rather, we stay in our partner's world, disciplining ourselves to stay present and see things as he or she does, according to how he or she remembers things. Everybody makes sense in their own world, and their feelings are legitimate. Listening well, therefore, puts us into the supportive position of being able to validate our partner's feelings. What they share with us in these dialogues is of vital importance if we desire to be intimately connected to them.

"In order to keep our attention on our partner, it may help to internally 'mirror' everything they say, to get and feel their meaning. We can take this even further and, at intervals, verbally repeat to them what we are hearing, or at least the essence of it, and ask them if we are 'getting it'. This outward mirroring, or paraphrasing, not only clarifies for us that we are understanding them as they want to be understood (which is what listening is all about); they receive the added comfort and feeling of safety of knowing that they are being heard. This helps and enables them to go deeper into their experience, revealing even more of their world to us, bringing a closer and more intimate connection. It also helps the sender understand themselves better and perhaps gain a new and objective perspective of their feelings as they hear them mirrored back."[43] Raymond and Furugh Switzer

Below is a summary of some pointers for positive sharing and listening experiences that demonstrate Trust and Dependability.

Before Starting

- Make sure the listener is available and attentive before beginning to speak; ask, "Is this a good time?"
- Minimize distractions like electronic devices or children having immediate needs

Ways of Communicating

- Start communications softly and gently
- Set aside biases, prejudices, and judgments

- Place Compassion in the forefront of our minds and hearts, so we can sincerely be understanding of our partner's inner world and life experiences
- Apply Compassion and Respect when asking questions to discern and understand the speaker's words, needs, feelings, fears, and concerns; one method: "We do this by asking cup-emptying questions starting with 'what,' 'when,' and 'how'—never 'why,' which puts each other on the defensive."[44] (Linda Kavelin Popov)
- Apply Self-Discipline to listen patiently without interrupting
- Listen attentively, summarizing understanding back to each other and clarifying the communication as needed
- Express caring and love as appropriate, sincerely encouraging our partner to share by using positive facial expressions, physical gestures, and brief words
- Speak for ourselves instead of our partner
- Interact in partnership and as teammates, working with a shared effort toward discerning truth and understanding one another better
- Sincerely affirm and demonstrate Respect toward our partner using positive and acknowledging words

Challenges

- Avoid words, tones of voice, or actions that communicate control, domination, or an adversarial position
- Take pause breaks when communication escalates toward dissension, arguments, or conflict
- Resume at an agreed time and place
- Set new goals for learning how to communicate and act with one another in improved ways

Despite all good intentions and hopes for a peaceful relationship or home, we may sometimes face difficult or hurtful communications. Each of us must apply Self-Discipline and Respect to govern our words and related behaviors. We can effectively observe how we either contribute to harmony or cause disunity. We remember that we are two adults and not parents to each other. As we observe our interactions, we can identify areas where improvement is needed.

When Words Cause Disunity

It's essential in maintaining our couple unity and well-being that we avoid any character attack, severe criticism, or harsh language, as these cause defensiveness, withdrawal, resentful feelings, and disunity. If these behaviors occur during conversations or consultations, they will interfere with achieving a positive outcome. Studies with couples at The Gottman Institute have observed some highly damaging behaviors that couples sometimes carry out and ways to behave instead. These are listed below:

1. **Criticism:** Negative words about personality or an attack on a partner's character; blaming a partner's personality or character for the problems in the relationship; example: "You are so irresponsible."

   How to fix it: Don't blame; use "I" instead of "you" to share your feelings and needs.

2. **Contempt:** Disregard and act superior through body language (examples: eye rolling, shrug, turning away...); or using sneering, sarcasm, patronizing, or self-righteous words; example, "You're such an idiot! Can't you do anything right?"

How to fix it: Hold positive thoughts and feelings; share admiration and appreciation.

3. **Defensiveness:** Resistant and blaming reaction; example, "I am not! You are always picking on me!"

 How to fix it: Accept responsibility for your actions.

4. **Stonewalling:** Withdrawal after repeated negative interactions, thereby exerting personal power to shut the partner out.

How to fix it: Take a pause break and then connect again.[45] Susanne M. Alexander and Johanna Merritt Wu

When we experience these four negative patterns, especially the first two, we can react at times with "flooding". This is a protective and anxious reaction, which has physical symptoms such as increased heart rate, higher blood pressure, sweating, and so on, overwhelming (flooding) us for about 20 minutes. It's then wise for us to stop communications completely to allow re-balancing, as communication becomes ineffective in this state.[46] Summarized from John Gottman and Nan Silver "... [T]here are severe limits on their ability to process information, to listen, to laugh, to be affectionate, to be empathetic, and to be creative. Thus, moderating physiological arousal is an important skill in conflict management."[47] John M. Gottman and Julie Schwartz Gottman

The Better Marriages organization recommends this approach below when anger arises between a couple.

1. "STOP! Do not attack. Anger creates defensiveness…and encourages counter-attacks, causing anger to increase and spread beyond the immediate issue.

2. "LOOK! Acknowledge anger. Couples make an agreement to view anger as a normal emotion. Each partner then agrees to acknowledge anger rather than suppress it, and to share how they feel with the other as soon as possible. Sharing is done with an 'I feel' statement…. Clarify with your partner how you interpreted what happened.

3. "LISTEN! Look behind the anger. Anger is typically a secondary emotion. The feelings labeled as anger are often deeper feelings—hurt, taken for granted, trapped, used, overloaded. Couples must look behind the anger…and deal with these other feelings if they are to manage anger. … When you get angry, consider what happened just before the incident? What else was I feeling (fatigue, hunger, frustration, overwhelmed, insecure, etc.)? Did this situation remind me of something in my background? Looking behind the anger may not be possible until emotions have 'cooled'. It's hard to think clearly and sort out feelings in the heat of a conflict. Silence or a 'time out' can be useful for a short period. But be careful that silence is not used as a weapon against your partner! Refusing to talk increases anger rather than resolving it. When tempers have cooled, partners can take turns stating what each is feeling while the other listens without interrupting. In this way, feelings can be clarified and heard."[48] "Creative Use of Conflict"

[See "Unifier 17: Resolving and Rebounding" for more assistance with this topic.]

Reducing Defensiveness

We can automatically react defensively when we hear a complaint or our partner raises an issue for consultation. However, we know that reaction makes it difficult to understand each other and solve problems. If we notice defensiveness beginning during any interaction, we can:

- Take a deep breath and release it slowly
- Recognize there's an opportunity to listen and learn by saying, "Can you tell me more about this?"; "Please help me to understand."; or something similar
- Summarize what we think we are hearing and understanding
- Clarify as needed
- Take a break to reflect and regroup, getting a snack or drink if it's helpful

"If defensiveness does arise, we may be able to communicate in this way:

- 'I hear you, and I would like to stick to what I brought up first.'
- 'Hey, did I sound critical? Let me try to say it again differently.'
- 'We're getting off-topic. Can we address this and talk about your concerns in a little while? Right now, I still want to address____.'
- 'I wonder if you feel defensive because of what I've said. Is that how you're feeling?'
- 'I'm talking about something important. Can we please stay on this topic?'"[49] Susanne M. Alexander and Johanna Merritt Wu

We can use wording that keeps us in learning mode and is less likely to trigger defensiveness. Below is a useful communication practice when we reflect together after trying new behaviors:

- "What worked well for me was ____, and I appreciated it very much."
- "What did not work as well for me was ____, and here is what might work better." Or, "Could we please consult about other solutions?"

This "X-Y-Z Formula" may also be useful when there's a complaint:

"In situation X, when you do Y, I feel Z. So instead of making a critical comment about [her husband's] driving, [a wife] learned to say, 'When we are driving down 4th Street with the kids in the back and you speed up to make the light, I sometimes feel like making the light is more important to you than our safety.' This simple way of phrasing a complaint is far less likely to cause problems than saying, 'You are such a reckless driver!'"[50] Les and Leslie Parrott

We can proceed with our consultation when we successfully reduce or eliminate defensive reactions. We can then build understanding and reach effective conclusions.

In everyday interactions at home, when we become aware, perhaps after hearing unhappy words, that our partner is struggling with fatigue, feeling overwhelmed, or facing another difficulty, we can prevent conflict with a constructive response. The recipient of the unhappy words could practice Compassion, take a deep breath, and not become defensive, instead saying, "How can I help?" Then, after some time of helping, communication can proceed.

Other Positive Approaches

As we have learned about and experimented with various methods for having honest and peaceful communication, we discovered the "Nonviolent Communication" approach. It's designed for people to share and receive observations, feelings, needs, and requests. The example below demonstrates "I-statements", where the speaker is careful to speak for themselves and not be accusatory with statements starting with "you". A simplified view of the basic communication process is:

- SEE: We observe and share the concrete actions in another person that affect our well-being.
- FEEL: We identify and share our feelings about what we observed.
- NEED: We notice and share the needs, values, desires, and so on that led to our feelings.
- REQUEST: We communicate (not demand) a specific request from the other person that's clear and positive, that if they carry it out, it will enrich our life. [To learn more, see Marshall Rosenberg, *Nonviolent Communication: A Language of Life*; https://www.cnvc.org/]

Here is an example: "I've noticed that you're getting involved in a lot of sports and exercise activities, and I appreciate your commitment to your health." I'm concerned, though, that we're spending less time together. I'm feeling lonely and missing you, and I'm frustrated that many tasks at home aren't being done. I value our relationship, and your time and attention greatly benefit our children. I request that we consult together before you pursue activities outside our home to ensure that we use Moderation and achieve balance together. After checking for understanding, a solution-seeking consultation can then follow.

Here is some encouragement about couple consultations:

"After the sender has conveyed all that is in their heart around the issue and has been heard and mirrored by the receiver, if the receiver then wants to respond to things that have been said, a conscious shift of roles is appropriate. This can go back and forth several times, if necessary, but it is important not to get muddled about who is in what role, so that listening is always taking place, protecting the safe and sacred space between husband and wife from the destructive effects of arguing back and forth.

"In summary, the goal of receiving is to understand completely the truth about what the other is experiencing, sensing, understanding, feeling, associating, remembering or fearing, and/or what she or he usually does when having such feelings, **and** to convey to the other with words, body language and tone of voice that we are 'getting them', that they are making sense (because all feelings are real and legitimate and everybody makes sense from their own point of view). A further goal is to imagine how they are feeling and empathize with them."[51]
Raymond and Furugh Switzer

If we reach an impasse in coming together reasonably, it may be wise for us to use outside assistance. We ensure that anyone we involve is strong in Dependability and will not take sides between us. Family members, for example, may find it easy to side with one of us.

Note: It's essential to receive professional assistance when feelings and interactions are seriously difficult and unresolved.

There's a difference between feelings that arise normally every day, or you have an occasional annoying interaction, rather than when the emotions are deep, serious, and stay for long periods. These are likely best addressed by a mental health professional.

Examples:

- "I love how much care you put into this project—could I please make a suggestion about it?"
- "I'm concerned about something. Could we sit and talk?"
- "I can see you're exhausted and hungry—I suggest we eat, relax, and talk later." [example of H.A.L.T.]
- "I apologize for trying to force a resolution. I would like to hear your ideas for addressing this issue."

Applying Virtues:

Below are some practical ways to incorporate virtues into daily practices with the theme of this chapter.

Compassion
- Know what is sensitive or hurtful to each other and proceed with care.
- Stay aware of what is happening in each other's life, and our fatigue and stress levels, and adjust our approach as needed.
- Reassure each other of our caring, even while raising difficult issues.

Respect
- Speak together as partners with equal voices.
- Appreciate and affirm each other's strengths and positive attributes, even while raising difficult issues.

- Listen attentively, summarize what was said, and use appropriate body language to show we are engaged in the consultation.

Self-Discipline

- Pause before speaking to think clearly about the message you want to deliver, and then move forward deliberately and carefully.
- Resist interacting based on negative feelings, look ahead to potential negative consequences of using harsh words, and apply Moderation to our approach and words.
- Calm our emotions, voices, and body language at the beginning and throughout communications to encourage feelings of safety and security for both of us.

Learning Activities:

1. Individually, observe and note when we say or do something that seems to prompt defensiveness or arguing from our partner. Assess whether the original communication included a critical tone of voice or attacking words. Become curious about what thoughts, feelings, or circumstances in our partner's life lead to this reaction. After there's greater understanding, apologize for any missteps. Set personal goals for reducing these behaviors. Then, practice, observe, and adjust as needed.

2. Consult and agree on several communication practices we commit to using consistently. We can begin compiling the list and continue adding to it over the next few weeks. Once we have a completed list, we can create a visual reminder to post in our home, on an electronic device, or both.

3. Obtain two large pieces of paper, one each, and a selection of various colored markers. Select a focus subject that's likely to be somewhat challenging for both of us. Use the markers on our papers to express our positive and negative feelings about the subject for an agreed-upon amount of time. The result can range from vigorous squiggles or slashes to something more artistic. Begin to consult about the topic by sharing our "drawings" and talking about what went through our minds during the activity.

4. Search the internet for and watch videos of Dr. John Gottman and other people speaking about the couples' research at the Gottman Institute.

5. To increase our skill in using kind words, we will attempt what researcher and author Shaunti Feldhahn has developed called a "30-Day Kindness Challenge" (www.shaunti.com). This will grow our understanding of how kind words and actions can transform a relationship. The Challenge has three aspects noted below.

   1. "Say nothing negative about your person, either to them or about them to someone else."
   2. "Every day, find one positive thing that you can sincerely praise or affirm about your person and tell them, and tell someone else."
   3. "Every day, do a small act of kindness or generosity for your person."

Feldhahn says that when these three aspects come together, they react and build "something remarkable, beautiful, powerful, and, above all, transformative."[52] Shaunti Feldhahn

Couple Reflection and Consultation:

Throughout this couple guide, there are invitations to practice the virtue of Reflection about your interactions and connection. This practice gives you opportunities to celebrate progress and consult to address issues.

1. What makes it easier for us to initiate interactions and conversations in a gentle and kind manner? (examples: preparation, maintaining well-being, conscious awareness, practice)
2. What benefits arise when an interaction begins with gentleness and kindness? How do we typically respond to one another?
3. What is the outcome for us when we begin an interaction harshly or with criticism?
4. What words, practices, and environment aid us in recovering and rebalancing into feeling like unified partners after difficult interactions? What aids us in remembering to speak and act differently next time?
5. What would assist us in distinguishing between a complaint and a criticism? How can we respond to complaints constructively?
6. How do we ensure we each fully share what is on our hearts and minds?
7. What assists us to listen without interrupting?
8. What are our preferred methods of communication?
9. Where are our favorite places for communication?
10. How do great communications make us feel?
11. How do excellent consultations make us feel?
12. How do we reconnect after a difficult communication? Are there better ways we prefer?

13. What specific actions will we take, or what personal growth efforts will we undertake, to enhance our communication skills?
14. What aspects of our communications do we want to monitor periodically? When will we reflect and consult about this?

Section 4:

Creating Connecting Experiences

Section 4 Introduction

Your connection as a couple is growing and becoming stronger. This section will now guide you through investing your time in activities that grow your unity and contribute to a thriving relationship. As you laugh, play, and have good quality time together, you will move closer to feeling "as one".

Thoughtfulness for each other's well-being and happiness leads you to practice Service with one another generously. Mutually applying Service increases your couple well-being.

The four Unifiers in this section will weave together your bodies, minds, hearts, and souls.

In Section 4, you will learn about and apply:

- Unifier 10: Choosing to Merge
- Unifier 11: Enjoying Social Time
- Unifier 12: Sharing Laughter and Humor
- Unifier 13: Giving Thoughtful Service

Unifier 10: Choosing to Merge

"A tendency to turn toward your partner is the basis of trust, emotional connection, passion, and a satisfying sex life."
John M. Gottman and Nan Silver

Focus Statement: We respond positively to one another's requests to share time, and we choose to initiate, deepen, and sustain our connections with one another, merging our lives.

Deeper Learning:

As we share experiences and live with each other, we develop patterns and habits that create a culture of how we respond to and connect. We seek opportunities to connect with one another and foster positive interactions. Our goal is oneness, where we achieve a union of our minds, hearts, bodies, and souls. Merging two lives isn't easy, and it can even be difficult and painful at times. Our commitment to staying connected helps us apply Perseverance throughout this merging process.

Here is a warning we are paying attention to:

"The natural drift of contemporary...life, in our busy, distracted, individualistic, consumer-driven, media-saturated, and work-oriented world, is toward less spark, less connection, less intimacy, and less focus on the couple relationship."[53] William J. Doherty

Being a couple provides us with companionship. We protect and enhance our relationship by paying attention and responding positively to each other's small and significant requests to share moments and experiences. Dr. John Gottman, a researcher of couples, has observed that couples connect and attune to one another when they turn toward each other, which fosters confidence and goodwill. These couples make minor and major "bids" for "each other's attention, affection, humor, or support." He and his coauthor indicate, "A tendency to turn toward your partner is the basis of trust, emotional connection, passion, and a satisfying sex life." Responding well to each other's "bids" then strengthens our connection.[54] John M. Gottman and Nan Silver

A request for connection from us can be somewhat indirect. We reach out to each other to draw notice to something to look at or share. We might share interesting information, tell a humorous story, or recount an experience we've just had. If our partner is engaged in an activity or distracted and working on an electronic device, the response can be minimal.

When we don't respond as we reach out to each other, we discourage connection and may hurt feelings. When we respond and engage with each other, unity grows, and we can merge our attention toward something together. The goal is to foster a sense of unity and partnership by sharing an experience. We may benefit from having our devices less present in some parts of our home, so we don't miss each other's bids to connect. We can also gently prompt our busy partner to look up, become present, and connect.

Sharing from Experience: *"My partner initially resisted learning about emotional bids for time. After I became upset, they ended up reading the material and making a conscious effort to engage with me in a different way. They offered words of appreciation every day. They also tried to listen for the feelings and emotions in the information I relayed, instead of just responding to the details. Now, when I share about my work, they ask follow-up questions about how I or my co-*

workers are feeling. Sometimes, they also offer support and sympathy, like saying, 'Wow! That sounds tough.'

"Now that a few weeks have passed, we are at a different place in our relationship and feel more connected. Today, I asked how it felt to offer emotional support using words, as I knew it was an effort and was sometimes uncomfortable. They said it felt like using new muscles and that some attempts felt like a wobble, trip, and fall. For me, it has also been a new experience—mostly positive—but I struggle at times with questions from my partner seeming intrusive. I need to remind myself to have patience and that with continued practice, we will find a better balance in this phase of our lives."

With practice and careful observation, thoughtfulness toward one another can deepen our connection. Attuning to each other can prompt us to notice when the other is likely to have a difficult day and take the necessary steps for support. We can notice when something the other person will enjoy becomes available. We can pick up a special gift or offer a delicious meal. The goal is to be thoughtfully aware of what opportunities for connection we will each appreciate.

One practice in a couple relationship that builds a strong connection is how we respond to good news from each other, no matter how small or large:

"Research shows that couples who regularly celebrate the good times have higher levels of commitment, intimacy, trust, and relationship satisfaction."[55] Tara Parker-Pope

Ways to respond could include showing enthusiasm and genuine interest, asking questions, expressing pride or appreciation, offering a hug, giving a gift, preparing a special meal, or spending quality time together.

Dr. William Doherty says intentional connection "rituals" are social interactions that are repeated, coordinated, and significant with a clear entry and exit. Actions don't count as a "ritual" if they don't significantly contribute to our closeness.[56] We have used this advice to establish rituals for greeting one another, communicating throughout the day, and engaging in activities together. Our activities include walking together once a week, watching a movie and eating pizza together every Friday evening, and cuddling at the end of each day. We treat special anniversaries as occasions to observe and celebrate.

Dr. Doherty says:

"What Leah [his wife] and I do during our talk ritual is an emotional check-in. It's 'How are you doing?' 'What has your day been like?' It's just a check-in. No problem solving, no logistics—just being friends savoring a brief interlude of personal conversation every day of their married lives."[57] William Doherty

Dr. Rob Skuka says there are three vital couple rituals: talking together for a minimum of 15 to 20 minutes each day, and if possible, including partner appreciation sharing; having a weekly in-depth dialogue for at least 30-60 minutes to focus on a significant issue, problem, or way to enhance the relationship; and having fun together.[58]

Sharing from Experience: *"My partner always makes coffee, tells me they love me when leaving for work, and kisses me even if we have disagreed the night before. An argument is a pothole in our marriage; it's not the whole journey. So, for us, the rituals are symbols that we are in this for the long haul, not just for the time an argument takes."*

When we spend time together away from our responsibilities, such as on a date or a vacation, we can focus on enhancing our friendship. This can include checking in on what is happening in each other's lives and any emotional responses to the situations we are facing. This check-in offers an opportunity to listen, be understanding, and provide support.

Dr. Doherty provides some guidelines for this check-in time together:

- There needs to be a clear transition into the time together and a clear exit
- If the activity involves a conversation, avoid logistics talk (who did or will do what, where, or when)
- Avoid problem-fixing talk
- Avoid conflict[59]

[More information about going on dates as a couple can be found in "Unifier 11: Enjoying Social Time".]

Sharing from Experience: *"We have developed a consistent practice in our marriage of checking in with each other periodically for updates. These maintain our close connection with one another. We can assess our progress and direction on decisions we have made related to a project, activity, or issue. We gain an understanding of each other's thoughts, feelings, desires, and beliefs when we ask open-ended questions in an encouraging and respectful tone of voice. Some examples of questions we use are:*

- *'How are you doing?'*
- *'How did your day go?'*
- *'How can I be supportive?'*
- *'What do you see are the next steps of our project?'*

- *'What unexpected demands are pressing on you that I should be aware of?'*
- *'What do you need from me, if anything, at this point?'*
- *'It will be a big day ahead for you. How do you feel?'*

"Consistent validations of virtues, a mindful presence, thoughtful observation, and prompt sharing keep us emotionally and spiritually connected. We make better decisions and avoid disunity. We are tuned into the pace and significant aspects of each other's lives as friends. This has been especially important for us when parenting young children and doing home renovation projects."

Checking in with each other may be done in person, but we also include text messages and calls, especially as we transition from one activity or place to another. As we greet and leave one another, our communications are also often in the form of a loving smile, a hug, a kiss—or all three!

We have daily opportunities for couple merging and growing a feeling of oneness between us. However, it can take time and repetition for a practice to feel comfortable and something to keep in our lives long-term. We started with a small number and gradually built up our practices until they became an integral part of our relationship's culture, making clear contributions to our unity.

Examples:

- Invite to see a sunrise, sunset, rainbow, moon, or stars.
- Share an article or something of interest.
- Request a listening ear.
- Exchange a hug, a kiss, or a touch before parting; greet each other after being apart.
- Send a text message and/or photo of what we are doing.

- Make our bed with fresh sheets together.
- Exercise together

Applying Virtues:

Below are some practical ways to incorporate virtues into daily practices with the theme of this chapter.

Creativity
- Initiate new ways to maintain close connections with one another.
- Take an action that we have used to connect with each other and alter it to happen in a new way.
- Play a game or engage in a fun activity that deepens our knowledge of each other.

Dependability
- Respond consistently and positively to each other's bids for connection.
- Work promptly, proactively, and diligently on high-priority issues.
- Seek help from and rely on one another.

Orderliness
- Create repeatable and routine habits that support us in consulting about important issues relevant to our relationship.
- Plan a longer amount of time together to allow for a deeper connection.
- Notice when an action has the potential to become a regular practice and systematically integrate it into our life.

Learning Activities:

1. Determine the "rituals" or practices that we enjoy and bring feelings of connection after being apart, and begin using them more regularly (examples: smiling, hugging, kissing, or simply sitting and talking for a few minutes).

2. Plan a regular time for us to talk each day or week while enjoying coffee, tea, a snack, or a meal. Carry it out consistently and assess how it's contributing to our connection.

3. Plan and carry out an enjoyable celebration of a current accomplishment one of us has had.

4. For an agreed amount of time, such as a week, carefully observe and respond to each other's bids for attention and connection. If a partner doesn't respond to an outreach, provide a gentle reminder. At the end of the time, consult about the effect on our relationship. Agree on what actions to continue.

5. Put on music that we both enjoy, and dance together in our home. Alternatively, we may enjoy music and dance in another location, or even take dancing lessons together.

6. Consult about the concept of oneness and merging to unite as a couple. How can we achieve this level of functioning while still feeling like we are unique individuals? What are the advantages to us of being merged into one?

Couple Reflection and Consultation:

Throughout this couple guide, there are invitations to practice the virtue of Reflection about your interactions and connection. This practice gives you opportunities to celebrate progress and consult to address issues.

1. What is our attitude about emotional bids for attention and connection? How do we generally respond to them?
2. When have we responded well to a bid for attention and connection?
3. When, if ever, does it feel like a problem or a burden to respond to each other's outreach in this way?
4. What do we celebrate in our lives? How do we celebrate?
5. If we don't currently do celebrations, what do we now want to start doing?
6. What are some of our favorite couple connection "rituals" or practices?
7. How do we feel when we consistently connect through a couple's "ritual"?
8. What connection practices do we want to increase, strengthen, or add?
9. When do we feel some resentment or resistance about what our partner invites us to do with them? What new approaches can we take to lessen resentment?
10. What are our views about concepts like "merging" and "oneness"?

Unifier 11: Enjoying Social Time

"Great dates involve communicating with one another,
reviving the spark that initially ignited your fire,
and developing mutual interests and goals...."
Claudia and David Arp

Focus Statement: We enjoy deepening our friendship and unity with fun and relaxing social experiences by ourselves and with others.

Deeper Learning:

Many relationship and marriage experts advise having dates with each other at all stages of life and experience. They encourage us to do this regardless of our financial or family circumstances. Our dates can often be inexpensive and allow us to spend time together when we can talk intimately. However, sometimes we choose to spend time and money planning and carrying out enjoyable activities, as we see it as a worthwhile investment. It's even possible for us to have a couple date at home once the children are asleep, but this isn't ideal as our children can wake up and interrupt us. This quotation is from one of our favorite experts on dates:

"We believe that having a healthy, growing marriage relationship requires friendship, fun, and romance. And there's no better way to encourage all of these things than having dates! Great dates are more than going to see a movie and tuning out the world for a while. Great dates involve communicating with one another, reviving the spark that initially ignited your fire, and developing mutual interests and goals that are not focused on your careers or your children. Great dates can revitalize your relationship."[60] Claudia and David Arp

Couple activities can assist us to stay current with each other's lives, help us be more supportive of each other, and reduce the chances of us ending our relationship. Dates are times when conversations and activities we both enjoy connect us on an emotional level. Keeping the dates interesting also contributes to connection and stress relief.

Sharing from Experience: *"We found that every date we had was just going to dinner at the same places, and that was getting boring. Now, we do Alphabet Dates each week, where we take turns and create a date that begins with a specific letter. It's a fun and surprising gift for our partner. Last week, I had the letter "B" and made a Bed of Blankets on the Beach, took Books along with us to read, and we had Breakfast for our evening meal. It's fun to spend the week thinking about what to come up with for the letter and have that to look forward to. We also appreciate that we each take the lead on the planning. Then, we share afterward what we enjoyed about the time together."*

We can demonstrate our commitment to quality time together by setting aside money for activities we enjoy. It can be tempting to focus solely on sacrificing for our children and handling our financial responsibilities, rather than also prioritizing quality time together. Balance is needed, and it assists us when we remember that the well-being of our home and family is founded on our well-being as a couple.

Time together can include a variety of options, such as:

• Having a meal in a restaurant or going on a picnic

- Talking on the phone or by video while one partner is away from home
- A spiritual gathering
- Exercising at the same time, such as going for a walk
- Doing a home maintenance project
- Watching a show or movie
- Attending a concert
- Playing a sport
- Engaging in sexual intimacy
- Going on a trip or vacation

We agree on our purpose for the activity and ensure that we include conversations that connect us and move our relationship forward.

Sharing from Experience: *"My partner enjoys going out to eat, so we do it sometimes when they suggest it. However, I'm beginning to realize that I have not been appreciating this time as a type of romantic interlude, as well as a place to eat dinner. Now I'm striving to improve our conversations when we go out, with fewer logistics and more relationship building."*

If we engage in activities together and end up feeling more distant, we reflect on and review what happened and why we feel this way. We then consult and agree on what to do differently the next time. It's also wise to minimize our social media use and screentime while doing an activity together to ensure we are focused on each other. If we notice increased screentime happening in our lives in general, we reflect and consult about why. It's good to assess if we are avoiding each other or if there are underlying issues that need to be addressed.

It can also grow our unity when we have social time, offering hospitality or spending time with friends who are couples, but this isn't the same as having our own couple time. The virtue of Moderation applies, so we also ensure we have time together on our own. [See more on involving others in "Unifier 19: Connecting with Friends and Community".]

Examples:

- Learning: museums, taking a course together
- Nature: boating, hiking, walking
- Exercise: swimming, biking
- Culture: concert, dancing
- Friends: picnic, shopping, sports

Applying Virtues:

Below are some practical ways to incorporate virtues into daily practices with the theme of this chapter.

Politeness and Sociability
- Include sharing stories about our lives, both past and present, as part of our social experiences.
- Invite others to our home to have positive experiences together.
- Build relationships with other couples so that we can share social time with them.

Orderliness
- Plan and arrange regular couple activities.
- Gather and organize the necessary resources for activities.
- Agree on boundaries for topics to consult about or avoid during couple social activities.

Positive Spirit

- Express enthusiasm for each other's ideas and plans for social activities.
- Sincerely enjoy spending time together socially.
- Share positive appreciation for each other when carrying out or completing a social activity.

Learning Activities:

1. Create and enjoy two Alphabet Dates, one planned by each partner. [See the story in the chapter for more information about these.]

2. Cooperatively plan a series of couple dates that include ones that take place at home and others that involve activities outside. Consider additional ones that we each plan separately as a surprise to the other, if we enjoy surprises. Consider what would make it possible to be more relaxed about a surprise plan.

3. Plan and carry out a short (1 to 4 days long) or a long (5 days or more) vacation that will include rest, relaxation, and social experiences together.

Couple Reflection and Consultation:

Throughout this couple guide, there are invitations to practice the virtue of Reflection about your interactions and connection. This practice gives you opportunities to celebrate progress and consult to address issues.

1. How happy or unhappy are we with the amount of couple time we have? What do we want to improve?
2. What activities do we enjoy doing on our favorite dates?

3. Can we have fun and be playful with each other during social events? What types of activities increase the likelihood of this occurring?
4. Is learning something new or learning about each other something we value in social circumstances? What types of activities increase the likelihood of this occurring?
5. What stories do we have about couple-time adventures?
6. How do we manage the expenses of social time? Can we improve our approach?
7. What arrangements for our children lead us to feeling relaxed, so we can enjoy our time away from them?
8. What are our couple friendships like? What new outreach do we want to do? What types of activities would we enjoy together with them?
9. What is our attitude toward offering hospitality as a means of connecting with others? What actions can we take to ensure the experience is unifying for us and positive for our guests?
10. How often do we take days away from home for a vacation experience? Do we need to do this more frequently or for a longer period? What are our favorite ways of doing this type of activity?

Unifier 12: Sharing Laughter and Humor

"Humor is about shared experiences
and a feeling of belonging."
Susan Sparks

Focus Statement: We prompt each other to laugh, use humor to respond to some of our challenges or irritations, and participate in enjoyable activities that lighten our lives.

Deeper Learning:

It's great when we can lighten up and laugh together to smooth our communications and unite us. We recognize there are many opportunities to be serious in our life, but we see no need to be sour-faced or perpetually solemn. Humor, happiness, and joy lift our spirits and contribute to our friendship.

Laughter is a choice, and it's an experience that begins when we are babies and children. However, as adults, we sometimes lose track of what brings us joy. At times, we think we are too grown-up to be silly and playful. Maybe it's time for us to lighten up a little.

"We view marriage [and relationships] as a commitment between two people to love, honor, cherish, and *entertain* each other.... ... You owe your partner a great deal of laughter...it's a mutual obligation. ... You didn't commit to one another in order to annoy and make each other miserable. Rather, you joined together because you hoped to make each other happier. ... [W]e are not suggesting that you constantly keep each other in stitches. The serious

and the routine are a part of all our lives. But these need to be punctuated with times of laughter."[61]
Jeanette C. Lauer and Robert H. Lauer

It can increase our unity when we are playful, humorous, and even entertaining with each other at appropriate times. This is also true when we spend time together relaxing and enjoying an activity or date. When we build connection in these ways, we more easily respond to whatever is going on in our lives. [See "Unifier 11: Enjoying Social Time".]

Genuine humor generates positive feelings and happiness throughout our shared life. One way we prompt laughter is to tell stories about our experiences. As we bring laughter to each other, it raises our happiness. We are then more likely to laugh with people throughout our lives.

One challenge with humor is that it can be misused. For example, if we pair laughter with sarcasm, ridicule, tromping on feelings, personal put-downs, or prejudice, we cause harm rather than produce joy and love. However, humor can take the form of gentle teasing as a way to accept each other's foibles or unique approaches to tasks. This lighter approach can prevent us from reacting with criticism or conflict.

We attempt humor at times that doesn't work as well as we want. Each person finds different things funny at times. One of us may laugh, while the other is baffled and doesn't get the joke at all. Sometimes, we may use humor as a means to shield ourselves from revealing our true feelings. The other person may then miss our point or not take it seriously. It takes courage to be more direct and not hide behind a laugh.

Sharing from Experience: *"When we began living together, every time I left the room briefly, my partner would turn the light off. I would go back into the room in darkness, which was very annoying. I realized this strong need to conserve electricity* *could be a source of regular conflict. Instead, we became playful about it. Sometimes, I turn the light off when my partner is still in the room. I tease them about whether they are getting anxious when they leave a light on unnecessarily. We joke about whether we can see in the dark. We now own amazing flashlights. Being 'light' about this has become an unexpected source of fun."*

Below are some insights about laughter, joy, and spirituality:

"Laughter is a spiritual practice. ... The transformative nature of any spiritual discipline comes with regular practice. When done consistently, it can eventually change our lives. If we make time to invite joy into our lives each day, we will become more aware of joy and laughter in our lives and in the world. Eventually, laughter will become an innate part of who we are."[62] Susan Sparks

"Cultivate humor as a higher path—a cosmic contentment that is truly lighthearted and full of joy. You will lighten the lives of others simply by the radiance of your good humor. Even the briefest laugh reminds us that we have available a kind of spiritual gold anytime, anywhere."[63] Stephen Post

Sharing from Experience: *"Laughter is healing medicine for the soul, mind, and heart. Laughter melts away imagined differences and brings to the forefront that we are all related in a very real way. It unites us. Joy, for me, is about detaching from the changes and chances of this world. Joy is kind to us and others. When I'm experiencing joy, I have more energy, I find life more pleasing and funnier in general. I'm better able to show compassion and empathize with others. I can serve* *others with grace and a cheerful attitude. I find it easier to think of others' needs and forget my selfish wants. People are happier around me when I'm happy and joyful!"*

The ability to laugh together and appreciate the humorous aspects of our lives can strengthen our relationship and family life. As one of us shares a story, laughter can spread to lift the spirits of our partner and out to family members and friends.

"It is a rare and beautiful quality to feel truly happy when others are happy. When someone rejoices in our happiness, we are flooded with respect and gratitude for their appreciation. When we take delight in the happiness of another, when we genuinely rejoice at their prosperity, success, or good fortune rather than begrudging it in any way, we are abiding in...sympathetic joy...."[64]
Sharon Salzberg

"Humor is about shared experiences and a feeling of belonging. It improves our mood through social connections. And when we feel less alone, we feel stronger."[65] Susan Sparks

Connecting through laughter, humor, and social time as a couple can:

- Increase the strength of our friendship
- Make it easier to cope with workload and difficulties
- Encourage and assist us and each other with personal growth and improvement
- Increase energy and productivity
- Deepen our emotional and physical intimacy
- Increase harmony and couple satisfaction
- Add balance to our busy lives

- Prompt us to relax and not take ourselves too seriously
- Remind us to feel grateful for our lives, each other, and family
- Assist us with building friendships with others

Sharing from Experience: *"One of the elements of our couple vision was to have a fun social time at least every few weeks. We kept struggling to carry it out, focusing instead on all the serious parts of our life. One day, we came across some research on the importance of couple connection, so we decided to take it seriously and have fun! We set up a folder and began saving money in it. When there was enough for an activity, we made specific plans and carried them out. We discovered that we liked spending time together this way!"* [See "Unifier 3: Where Are We Going?" about visioning.]

Our ability to enjoy being with each other, regardless of the circumstances, is powerful in keeping us connected.

Examples:

- Watch a comedy show, play, or movie
- Gently tease each other about something silly
- Share a funny story from an experience
- Create a couple date that maximizes laughter

Applying Virtues:

Below are some practical ways to incorporate virtues into daily practices with the theme of this chapter.

Creativity
- Seek new ways to consciously encourage laughter between us.

- Develop a new method for assisting one another to relax.
- Share stories regularly.

Moderation
- Know when to be humorous and when to be serious.
- Balance our life with regular humor.
- Laugh *with* each other, not *at* each other.

Positive Spirit
- Maintain positivity, optimism, and enthusiasm even when things become difficult.
- Use humor in ways that uplift each other and diffuse tension.
- Rise above immediate emotional distress or annoyance at each other's quirks, keeping in mind the long-term happiness in the relationship.

Learning Activities:

1. **Building Storytelling Skills:** One of us shares a story, pausing every few sentences to allow the listener to ask a question or make a summarizing statement that checks for understanding. Take time to clarify if we don't completely understand each other. At the end of the story, the listener summarizes and shares:

    a. What seemed to be important from the speaker's experience?
    b. What feelings did the speaker seem to experience? (examples: anger, sadness, happiness, frustration, excitement...).
    c. How they felt while listening to the story: What was the effect of this story on them? What moved, touched, or inspired them?

   d. Were there any humorous aspects to the story that they enjoyed?

2. **Building Sharing Humor Skills:** The action components below can be carried out just with each other or with other people involved. After each story or joke, the listeners share what was funny (or not) to them, how they responded to the humor, and what they learned.

   a. Funny stories about the relationships or marriages of our parents, grandparents, other relatives, or friends.
   b. Funny stories about our couple relationship or family life.
   c. Funny stories from a recent (or childhood) experience.
   d. Jokes or puns.

3. Consult about an interaction we have repeatedly had about something that annoys us but is unlikely to change, and then determine a way to respond with humor and playfulness instead.

4. Find and share a video, movie, or comedy show to discover what makes each of us laugh. If one of us doesn't find the item funny, search for material we both respond to with laughter.

Couple Reflection and Consultation:

Throughout this couple guide, there are invitations to practice the virtue of Reflection about your interactions and connection. This practice gives you opportunities to celebrate progress and consult to address issues.

1. How do we feel when we laugh? What often makes each of us laugh?
2. Can we share stories with each other? What would remind us to do this activity more often?
3. Do we joke or tease in a way that seems to uplift each other?
4. What prompts us to be fun and playful with each other? How do we feel about behaving this way?
5. When have laughter and humor increased our unity with one another? Built friendships with other people?
6. When has humor made us feel more distant from one another? Do we ever use humor in a way that may be hurtful, such as speaking with sarcasm or poking at sensitive areas? What would guide or support us in forming new behaviors?
7. How do we respond to physical humor? To intellectual humor?
8. What activities might prompt us to laugh more and feel like we're having fun together?
9. Do we see a link between laughter and maintaining peace between us? Is there a link to passion?

Unifier 13: Giving Thoughtful Service

*"Requests are a means to develop
the kind of partnership that takes into account
each other's needs, wants, and desires."*
Sandra Gray Bender

Focus Statement: We communicate our wishes and needs, and we apply Service to fulfill them for each other.

Deeper Learning:

Over time, through mutual communication and encouragement, we develop an awareness of the words and actions we can offer that benefit each other. With practice, we increasingly fulfill each other's needs by providing our Service. When we receive this offering from each other, it feels like receiving love, and we express sincere appreciation.

While it's great to anticipate each other's needs, we often struggle to do so. It's a mistake if we think that if our partner loves and cares about us, they should automatically know what we need. To sort out all of this and maintain a balanced relationship, we must regularly consult to determine the best course of action. We must also consider what we are capable of and what we are not, as well as what others can do to assist us. We give each other the grace of words and make requests of each other, and then we do our best to show Compassion and be thoughtful and considerate in response. [See more about avoiding mind-reading in "Unifier 5: Understanding Each Other".]

"... [O]ne aspect of the partnership is determining what each will do for the other. Requests are a means to develop the kind of partnership that takes into account each other's needs, wants, and desires."[66] Sandra Gray Bender

We maintain reciprocity as we apply the virtue of Service within our relationship and family. This prevents or eliminates destructive self-centered or selfish behavior patterns. Here is a perspective on this dynamic:

"The antidote to selfishness is service. It is difficult to be selfish when you are serving your spouse. Service forces you to put the needs of your spouse in front of your own needs. One of the keys to a strong marriage lies in fulfilling your spouse's needs before your own. When you use this key, a spirit of service will soon permeate your relationship. This spirit of service is contagious."[67] "Marriage, Increase the Joy, Decrease the Misery"

When we offer Service to each other, we create a culture where both of us feel satisfied and cared for. Naturally, we have personal needs that we must look after ourselves. However, when we can assist each other, it strengthens our Trust and increases our love for one another. For example, one of us might need time alone to recharge energy batteries, and our partner notices the fatigue level, encourages rest, and takes on some extra tasks.

Sharing from Experience: *"What I love about our relationship is that we both regularly practice Service with each other in kind, courteous, and thoughtful ways. These actions smooth the rough edges of life and help us appreciate each other. Fixing a meal, holding a door open, setting the table, getting the mail, providing a glass of water, checking the functioning of a vehicle, bringing a small gift, massaging a neck, offering* *reminders, and more all help our relationship and home flow more smoothly and peacefully."*

However, we also know that busyness, distraction, health issues, and other limitations can sometimes make it difficult to see and fulfill each other's needs. Disunity and difficulties can arise when we fail to share, recognize, or meet key expectations and needs. Willard Harley observes in his work that people will often violate even their own most fundamental values to meet their perceived needs. Recognizing and meeting one another's needs is one of many ways to prevent the unhappiness, resentment, relationship breakdown, and infidelity that can result from consistently unmet needs. Harley says:

"Often the failure of men and women to meet each other's emotional needs is simply due to ignorance of each other's needs and not selfish unwillingness to be considerate. Fulfilling those needs does not mean you have to painfully grit your teeth, making the best of something you hate. It means preparing yourself to meet needs you may not appreciate yourself. By learning to understand your spouse as a totally different person than you, you can begin to [meet] that person's emotional needs."[68]
Willard F. Harley, Jr.

When we understand each other's primary needs, we identify the highest priorities for action. Our union is likely to be stronger and happier when we meet these needs to the best of our ability. We apply Moderation, give thoughtful attention, and ensure we are both actively engaged. As we realize our own needs are met, we feel stronger and more able to reach out and meet our partner's needs. It's wise to periodically re-examine our relationship to ensure we are recognizing and meeting each other's most vital needs, as well as those that contribute to the quality of each other's life.

As our union grows and matures, significant events related to children, work, or our health prompt us to review our needs and whether to prioritize them. We can also establish a practice of asking each other what we can do to help them immediately.

Sharing from Experience: *"For years my wife Keri and I struggled. … [O]ur personalities didn't quite match up. And the longer we were married the more extreme the differences seemed. … Our fighting became so constant that it was difficult to even imagine a peaceful relationship. We became perpetually defensive, building emotional fortresses around our hearts. We were on the edge of divorce and more than once we discussed it.*

"Through time I've learned that our experience was an illustration of a much larger lesson about marriage. Everyone in a committed relationship should ask their significant other, 'What can I do to make your life better?' … Real love is … to expand our capabilities of tolerance and caring and actively seek another's well-being. All else is simply a charade of self-interest."[69] *Richard Paul Evans*

We benefit from identifying our needs as a couple and strive to create solutions for them. For example, these needs could include social time, hospitality, or sexual intimacy. We focus on addressing the elements that create a harmonious relationship and household. When this harmony exists, we can feel secure and more easily reach out to apply Service to meet the needs of family members and people beyond our home.

Some examples of practicing thoughtful Service to each other are listed below.

- Offering and fixing something to drink or eat
- Washing clothes that the other person needs for an activity or event
- Bringing a gift that uplifts the other through a difficult time
- Looking after young children so the other can rest
- Arranging a date or social occasion
- Fixing something in the home that's a safety hazard
- Initiating physical intimacy if there's openness to it
- Massaging a sore part of the body
- Listening carefully to what is shared

It's naturally challenging to meet each other's needs consistently. Life is full of adventures, and there are often disruptions in the flow between us due to work requirements, meeting the needs of children or family members, illness, and other life events. It's unreasonable and unrealistic to expect any partner always to meet all one's needs and expectations. We can do our best, but it's wise to avoid thinking that we are in serious trouble when we cannot be perfect at this. Using Reflection and consultation are vital, so we can determine what works well for both of us. In this process, we consider:

- When sacrifice is an appropriate choice,
- When Moderation is needed, and
- When to apply Creativity to develop alternatives.

Here is a reflection on expectations:

"In general, you will be disappointed or happy in life depending on how well your perceptions of what is happening match what you expected—what you think should be happening. It's not surprising, therefore, that expectations play a crucial role in how happy your marriage will be. ... [I]t may not be as crucial for the two of you to hold all the same expectations as it is for each of you to do your best to try to meet the important (and realistic) desires of the other."[70]   Howard J. Markman, Scott M. Stanley, and Susan L. Blumberg

As we grow as individuals, we learn when it's great to acknowledge or celebrate our practice of Service to each other and when it's fine if there's little or no response. The genuine practice of Service doesn't seek credit, because it's a gift to the recipient. We serve one another out of love and care, not out of a desire to be noticed and praised.

Sharing from Experience: *"Practicing service within my family is all about everyone working together to set everyone else up for good outcomes. There are many small things that I do regularly to set my partner up for success, rather than failure, without making them feel belittled or micromanaged. Most services that I provide to my partner are completed without them ever realizing that I am doing them. There's usually no appreciation beyond my seeing the result, which is all that's usually necessary for me."*

Caution: Due to a traumatic experience or psychological or emotional problems, some partners may feel they don't deserve to have needs, communicate them, or have them met. In other cases, partners can adopt a selfish attitude of entitlement, believing their needs are more important. Yet others may blame themselves or others for unmet needs. Partners can contribute to healing these perceptions. However, some people may also need professional assistance.

Remember, too, that healthy individuals also have a responsibility to maintain their own well-being and happiness. While couples support each other, individual partners cannot expect someone else to "make" them healthy or happy. Most couples also discover that people other than a partner can effectively meet some of their needs, such as close friends. Remember that it's wise to agree on who is meeting the needs outside of each other, so there's no harm to the relationship.

Examples:

- Preparing a beverage or food for the other.
- Obtaining clothing for a special occasion.
- Consulting about a work problem.
- Providing energy recharge time and space.
- Saying a prayer for each other.
- Buying groceries.
- Planning a trip and making reservations.

Applying Virtues:

Below are some practical ways to incorporate virtues into daily practices with the theme of this chapter.

Politeness and Sociability
- Respond to each other's requests and needs with warmth and generosity.
- Make ourselves available to listen, share, encourage, and accompany each other through whatever arises.
- Listen to each other to understand and develop shared interests and activities.

Humility
- Stop our activities to focus on each other's wishes or needs.

- Acknowledge how valuable our partner's well-being is to the relationship.
- Respond willingly and positively to requests for our attention or help.

Service

- Notice and thoughtfully consider what to give to and receive from each other, and carry out the best actions possible.
- Listen attentively and determine what each of us is truly communicating and what we truly need.
- Confidently initiate positive actions, believing that loving actions can significantly contribute to the quality of our relationship.

Learning Activities:

1. Reflect together on our primary needs and how they can be met using the list below, which is in no order. Choose the top three that are most important to each of us. Consider such items as:

   - Affection, Connection, and Love
   - Admiration and Significance*
   - Sexual Fulfillment
   - Financial Income and Management
   - Conversation
   - Recreational Companionship
   - Spiritual Companionship
   - Partnership
   - Resolution
   - Openness
   - Attractiveness

- Domestic Support
- Marriage/Partner Commitment
- Spontaneity and Variety
- Family Commitment
- Certainty and Security
- Personal Growth
- Humor, Laughter, and Lightness
- Being of Service71

* The explanation of "Admiration and Significance" is: "Respects, values, and appreciates me, helping me feel special and unique as a person and as a partner; makes negative comments only rarely and then with kindness; acknowledges my accomplishments; expresses admiration to me clearly and often." Susanne M. Alexander

2. Consult and identify two new ways we can demonstrate Service to each other. Carry them out and reflect on the outcome.

Couple Reflection and Consultation:

Throughout this couple guide, there are invitations to practice the virtue of Reflection about your interactions and connection. This practice gives you opportunities to celebrate progress and consult to address issues.

1. What are our beliefs and attitudes about demonstrating Service to each other?
2. In what ways do we show that meeting each other's needs is important to us?
3. What areas in our lives may have become unbalanced, with one of us doing much more for the other, our family, and around our home than the other? What will we

adjust in this situation? [Be cautious not to criticize or blame.]

4. How do we address situations in which our needs are not being met as well as we want?

5. How could we handle a situation where one of us firmly insists that the other carry out actions that would likely benefit us, but that they are unwilling or unable to do?

6. If we don't show a positive attitude when serving each other, how do we feel about the actions we receive?

7. What needs could we thoughtfully meet for each other that we are not currently doing?

8. Are we doing any actions that we believe demonstrate Service, but they are unwise as they interfere with our partner's ability to take responsibility?

9. How does our example of demonstrating Service to each other provide a model for others, such as our children or friends?

10. When do we feel resistant or resentful about offering thoughtful services?

11. What services do we find bring us joy and delight to give and receive from one another?

12. What types of services build physical, mental, emotional, or spiritual intimacy?

Section 5:

Forging Deeper Connection

Section 5 Introduction

As you navigate more sensitive topics, and as you learn and grow your unity together through challenges, you forge a deeper connection with one another.

Sexual intimacy is a key area of union for a couple. However, being able to talk about what you appreciate, and your skillfulness in working through challenges with sex, demonstrate your maturity and strength.

Your personal experiences and attitudes toward money influence how you perceive and manage it. Unity grows as you understand each other's viewpoints, consult, and come to unified agreements on how to manage money.

Throughout your life together, you will always face challenges to overcome, new skills to acquire, and forgiveness to cultivate. You will grow and develop as individuals and as a couple. Opportunities will arise to reclaim unity when it slips and resiliently rebound from difficult times.

In Section 5, you will dive deeper into:

- Unifier 14: Communicating About Sex
- Unifier 15: Managing Our Money
- Unifier 16: Growing from Difficulties
- Unifier 17: Resolving and Rebounding

Unifier 14: Communicating About Sex

"Emotional connection creates great sex,
and great sex creates deeper emotional connection."
Sue Johnson

Focus Statement: We value the physical intimacy that happens in the context of our emotional intimacy and love, and we share thoughts and feelings about our sex life to build deeper understanding, determine new actions, and strengthen our connection.

Deeper Learning:

We create our sexual and sensual experiences together. It builds our connection when we share what types of touch and experiences we value, and which ones are best to modify or do very differently. This dynamic, mutual sharing can enhance our experiences and create a more profound sense of oneness.

Our experiences and the responsiveness of our bodies will vary over time and in changing circumstances. However, our ability to consult through any challenges that arise will enhance our ability to keep physical touch as a key element that unites us. Here are some insights:

"There are two key factors related to satisfying sex: emotional connection and conversations about sex. The second one often gets overlooked, but research shows that only 9% of couples who can't talk comfortably about sex report sexual satisfaction. By talking about sex, couples develop a 'script' or 'playbook' for how to please one another emotionally and sexually. ... That's why it's vital for couples to not only prioritize sex in the relationship, but also to learn how to talk about sex comfortably on a consistent basis. How can you make it more comfortable? Sharing your likes and dislikes about sex isn't a difficult task in itself, but being that vulnerable (even with your soulmate!) can make it a very difficult task. To make it more comfortable, try to think about sex as a physical expression of your friendship. At its core, the goal of sex is to become closer friends and have fun together. This reframing makes it a friendship issue, which is easier to address than a sexual issue."[72] Get Lasting

There is a link between sex and emotional connection:

"... [S]ecure bonding and fully satisfying sexuality go hand in hand; they cue off and enhance each other. Emotional connection creates great sex, and great sex creates deeper emotional connection. When partners are emotionally accessible, responsive, and engaged, sex becomes intimate play, a safe adventure. Secure partners feel free and confident to surrender to sensation in each other's arms, explore and fulfill their sexual needs, and share their deepest joys, longings, and vulnerabilities. Then, lovemaking is truly making love."[73] Sue Johnson

Our ability to share honestly and listen lovingly about such a personal topic can enhance our experiences. [You have been learning about meeting each other's needs throughout this book, including in "Unifier 7: Loving One Another" and in "Unifier 13: Giving Thoughtful Service".]

Success Factors

There's a time and place for everything, including consultations about sex and touch. These are usually best if we are in a private place where we will not be interrupted, and we can truly hear what is on each other's minds. We have learned that we should be gentle with our honesty:

"Discussions about sexual issues should come from a place of love and from a wish for maximizing the sexual experience for both of you. When you bring up the subject, here are a few tips to get what you want out of the discussion:

- Be direct...
- Use humor...
- Start with a positive...."[74] Scott Haltzman

While we are often comfortable talking about our sexual intimacy, sometimes it does become difficult. We must remain aware of how our words impact one another. We are often very sensitive about topics related to our bodies and how they function, as well as our preferences related to touch. Our consultations must be affirming, encouraging, and loving.

Compassion is a wise and supportive virtue when discussing what we like or dislike about each other's actions or what might be missing from our sexual experiences. As we share about our own bodies and emotions and raise our concerns, we can then see the situation from our partner's perspective. We accompany each other, and we do our best to be sensitive with our requests and enthusiastic in response to fun suggestions we both appreciate.

Sharing from Experience: *"When we first became a serious couple, we talked about our sexual histories more than our preferences. This was important in helping us understand each other and our responses. Now we tend to focus more on our preferences.*

"Over the years of experiencing touch, learning what is sensitive to each of us, and observing responses to different experiences, we can usually sense if an experience is good or when there's something to talk about. We have learned not to initiate consultations in the middle of experiences, as that seems to derail our involvement and arousal. Later, we can talk about what went well, what we would have preferred, and what is something new to try.

"On such a sensitive topic, we are careful to avoid any words that seem critical or that might prompt the other to feel insecure or devalued. We are careful to affirm to each other that our intimate experiences are something we value, and we are consulting about them to enhance our experiences."

We have noticed that sometimes we cannot immediately respond to what each other raises, because it's such a personal topic. Sometimes, we react emotionally, and it takes a few hours or days to be clear about our thoughts and feelings. This delay may be especially true if the topic reminds us of difficult experiences in the past. It's helpful to notice and share when something that happened previously is affecting us in the present.

Enhancing Experiences with Virtues

Our virtue strengths influence the quality of our consultations about sex. They also influence the quality of our sensual and sexual experiences. Virtues such as Flexibility, Respect, Creativity, and Trust assist us to explore and learn each other's sensual and sexual preferences. These virtues also contribute to our connection:

"A spiritual relationship is the radiant result of mutually expressed compassion. The connection happens on all levels—emotional, intellectual, sensual, and sexual. It's a powerful resonance that emanates from one soul's recognition of another. This is the best kind of relationship, and it engenders the absolute best kind of sex. When you have this kind of union, intercourse becomes much more than physical pleasure. It's alive with waves of appreciation and bone-tingling love. When the joy is centered in the heart—not just in the genitals—there's nothing else like it!"[75] Sandra Anne Taylor

Sharing from Experience: *"Touching each other deeply fulfills our need for love and caring. Often, we blend our physical, emotional, and spiritual feelings toward each other. We view sexual intimacy as a way to joyfully connect."*

Virtues that assist us in being intimate include Adherence and Dependability, which are vital components of the "attachment circuitry" that supports commitment and faithfulness to one another:

"... [T]he first condition for a healthy and truly satisfying sexual connection is a commitment, with absolute faithfulness, to a relationship that will endure.... [I]t is the attachment circuitry, which comes into play in the long-term commitment of a couple to each other, that brings the greatest amount of sexual satisfaction."[76]
Raymond and Furugh Switzer

Physical Factors

Sexual functioning is biologically complex. When we're unsure about how our bodies function, we find it helpful to learn from and consult with specialists on the topic. We discovered this key insight in our reading:

> "... [F]or some people, sexual desire—the urge to become sexual—doesn't *precede* feeling aroused; it actually follows it. In other words, some people rarely (or never) find themselves fantasizing about sex or feeling sexual urges, but when they're open to becoming sexual with their spouses anyway, they often find the sexual stimulation pleasurable, and they become aroused. Once aroused, there is a desire to continue. And that's every bit as much 'sexual desire' as the more traditional view of things."[77] Michele Weiner Davis

We also see and understand that our bodies change regularly, including from fluctuating hormones, illness, injury, and aging, and this affects our sex life.

Sharing from Experience: *"As our bodies change throughout life, we notice a need for Flexibility, Humility, cooperation, and understanding. Lightening up with humor can sometimes contribute to gentle acceptance of what we cannot change. We also see how important it is to stay as physically fit as possible."*

Here are some further thoughts:

> "The major functions of marital sexuality are a shared pleasure, a means to deepen and strengthen intimacy, and a tension reducer to deal with the stresses of life and marriage. ... There are myriad ways of being sexual. ...

Sometimes sex can be long, tender, warm, and involving (like a four-course gourmet dinner). Other times sex can be short and lusty (like a hamburger and fries). Marital sex is a mix and match depending on your feelings, needs, and practical and time constraints. If all sex were 'quickies' or a 3-hour lovemaking experience, it would become boring. Sexuality can be intimate or playful, a late-night way to end the day or a middle-of-the-day main event, a way to reconnect after a conflict, or a pleasant reassurance. The essence of creative sexuality is awareness of your feelings and needs with freedom to communicate desires and share with your spouse.

"The prescription for satisfying marital sex is integrating emotional intimacy, nondemand pleasuring, and erotic scenarios and techniques. These will not be present at each experience but are the foundation for healthy marital sexuality."[78] Barry and Emily J. McCarthy

Caution: When sharing with each other about your couple sexual experiences, your goal is to practice Compassion. This assists you to listen, understand, and find new approaches that are acceptable for both of you to try. If you're frustrated in this process, you may need to seek assistance from a specialist in the field, or through books, videos, or counseling.

You may also need to seek medical or counseling support if something is interfering with your experiences, such as pornography or fetishes, previous trauma, addictions, attraction to someone else, or physical or emotional impairment. Mid-life physical changes can raise challenges, such as vaginal dryness or erection issues. You may find it helpful to consult with professionals and try medications, supplements, or specific exercises.

Examples:

- "I find it difficult to breathe and relax when you're fully on top of me. I wonder what different positions we could try?"
- "It arouses me when you touch me in these ways and places: ____. Are you willing to try these?"
- "What could I do that would bring you greater pleasure?"
- "It doesn't concern me that a climax/orgasm didn't happen, but I do feel hurt that you turned away from me afterward. Could we please talk about this?"
- "Could we experiment with trying ____ next time?"
- "I'm frustrated that we are having sex less often, and I'm also concerned about why. Can you please share with me what seems to be happening?
- "Hearing the kids in the other room put the brakes on my arousal and response to you. What can we do to help me with this? Would intimacy with different timing be possible?"

Applying Virtues:

Below are some practical ways to incorporate virtues into daily practices with the theme of this chapter.

Compassion
- Understand the sensitive nature of each other's history with sexual experiences and touch.
- Observe and respond with loving-kindness when either of us has a challenge with performance or limitations.
- Approach a resumption of sensual or sexual activity after a time of necessary abstinence with advance consultation and with care and gentleness.

Trust
- Consult about sex carefully, demonstrating Respect for each other's sensitivities and challenges.
- Maintain faithfulness to one another in words and actions.
- Demonstrate confidence in each other's goodwill intentions and gestures of affection and touch.

Truthfulness
- Share what we each believe about what is happening and why.
- Avoid making assumptions, and proceed to bravely raise requests and concerns, believing that there may be new options to try.
- Patiently communicate acceptance of circumstances and functioning that cannot be changed.

Learning Activities:

1. Hold hands and walk in an attractive area of nature. Take turns talking generally about our sexual intimacy experiences together. Agree on one new action, carry it out privately, and reflect on the experience together. Note: This arrangement may contribute to you feeling safely connected, and reducing eye contact may make the conversation more comfortable.

2. Choose two or three virtues to incorporate into our sexual experiences regularly.

3. Experiment with different frequencies for our sexual experiences and assess our responses to the timing. What are our preferences regarding frequency? How can we adjust when there are differences with this?

4. Consult about our timing for sexual intimacy:
   a. Are we being spontaneous? Planning for our time together? Doing a combination of both?
   b. What could contribute to us being more successful? (examples: the location, nearness of people, time of day, lock on the door...)

Couple Reflection and Consultation:

Throughout this couple guide, there are invitations to practice the virtue of Reflection about your interactions and connection. This practice gives you opportunities to celebrate progress and consult to address issues.

Note: These consultations may be difficult and emotional. You can pause after reading each question to use your Reflection individually and then begin to share, taking turns as appropriate. It's wise to carefully avoid assuming what each of you will say and stay open to fully listening without interrupting. Breathe deeply and take breaks as needed.

1. What makes it easier for us to talk about our sex life?
2. What do we consider the primary purposes of sex? Of sensual touch?
3. When does sexual intimacy feel most unifying to us? How could we increase the feeling of oneness between us during physical and sexual intimacy?
4. What are our views about how our thoughts, emotions, and spiritual connection affect our sexual intimacy? What would increase our connection related to sex?
5. What types of negative interactions between us affect the frequency or quality of our sexual experiences? How do our stress levels affect our experiences?

6. What enhances our sexual pleasure? What interferes with it?
7. How or when is cleanliness a significant factor in our experiences? Do we need to increase cleanliness to enhance intimacy?
8. What do we most appreciate about each other's bodies and sexual actions and responses?
9. What prompts arousal in each of us? How can we assist each other to feel aroused? What causes arousal and involvement in the experience to slow down or stop?
10. What specific experiences do we each have in mind? Are we willing or able to try accommodating these? What would make it easier for us to relax about carrying them out?
11. What types of touch or experiences are we uncomfortable with or directly request not happen?
12. At times when sexual intimacy isn't possible, but we still want to be touched, what types of touch do we prefer?
13. Would we benefit from learning more about how male and female anatomy and physiology work? What are good sources of accurate information? (Please consider *Come As You Are* by Emily Nagoski.)
14. Are there issues for us with infidelity through pornography or contact with someone else emotionally or in person who is outside of our couple relationship? How are we addressing the situation? What more do we need to do?
15. Are there experiences from before our relationship that were negative or abusive that are affecting either of us now? How are we addressing these?
16. What indications suggest that we may need help from professional services, a support group, or both?

Unifier 15: Managing Our Money

"Taking the time to figure out what's really going on when there are money conflicts will make your relationship richer, more compassionate, and more successful."
Syble Solomon

Focus Statement: We view money as a resource entrusted to us to manage wisely, and we strive to agree on how we and others responsibly manage our finances—earning, saving, investing, and sharing money in alignment with our values.

Deeper Learning:

As we consult about and manage our finances effectively, we see how money aligns with our unified vision and connection efforts. We view money as a valuable resource, and we strive to earn what is necessary, spend and give responsibly, consider the well-being of all family members, and plan for savings and investments to support our short-term and long-term future. Our well-managed finances are part of having a flourishing family. [See "Unifier 3: Where Are We Going?" about visioning.]

Many couples sometimes struggle with topics related to money, including us. Managing finances can be complex, and it's in grappling with that complexity that we grow and deepen our relationship. To protect our unity, we ensure that we consult about all decisions that involve our finances. We also keep each other fully and regularly informed about the actual state of our finances and how to access our resources. We review our documents, reports, and plans as needed and when circumstances in our life change.

[*Caution:* Be cautious about sharing financial and password information and making important financial decisions before entering a seriously committed relationship or marriage.]

Our History and Values

We have layers of emotional memories related to money, which often lead to power and control issues in managing and using it. The values and beliefs we each hold about earning an income, spending, saving, giving, investing, and managing money are often linked to experiences in our homes growing up and as adults before our relationship began. These values and beliefs from earlier in life may contribute to couple harmony or be quite divergent. The goal as a couple is to consult and agree on a shared set of values and practices that we will each adhere to as best we can.

There may also be history from early in our relationship when we were less skillful, which still affects us today. Often, our experiences and observations related to money, both from our childhood and in our relationship, cause us to act or react automatically to money experiences now.

When a disagreement arises between us, it's good to do fact-finding that includes a gentle inquiry about why the issue seems so emotionally charged. Syble Solomon, an expert on financial habits and the psychology of money, suggests the following to couples:

"Money is a complex topic and pushes more hot buttons than any other issue in a relationship. When money seems to be the cause of conflict, it's a good time to step back, take a deep breath, and give yourselves some space. This time-out will help you to discover what's really going on. ... Money represents power, control, freedom, success, security, acceptance, status, love, and many other strong emotional needs. These needs may be associated with memories that can be pleasant, hurtful, exciting, or scary. These needs and memories often cause you to react strongly to what seems to be a money issue in your relationship. ... Taking the time to figure out what's really going on when there are money conflicts will make your relationship richer, more compassionate, and more successful."[79]

Sharing from Experience: *"When we were dating, I wanted to make a big deal about Valentine's Day [a North American holiday that encourages expressions of affection], but my partner did not. I had gone many years as a single person without someone to share the day with. However, my partner had worked for a florist one Valentine's Day, and the materialism involved with spending money to express love truly bothered them. We had a sincere consultation about this, and we decided that we could both agree to exchange romantic cards. We don't purchase gifts, decorate, or make it a special day in the family with certain foods and gifts for the children. Our children receive Valentine's Day cards from their grandparents and participate in card exchanges at school. We both treasure the cards we exchange, our children see our loving words, and we have not invested in the materialism that certain 'holidays' have become.*

"Because we realized that we had both come to our marriage with expectations, in the first few years, we thought about how we wanted to celebrate special calendar days and what types of money we wanted to spend on them. We decided that birthdays were a special day for each member of the family, and we would celebrate with a special meal, gifts, a trip to the museum, or a movie. We decided that we would not exchange gifts on our wedding anniversary, but instead, we would buy something for our home together, which we have

enjoyed. *Every five years, we buy tickets to a play or opera we really want to see. This has brought us much pleasure. By consulting together early in our marriage about holiday expectations, we have been able to craft a family culture that emphasizes events, activities, and expressions of caring rather than possessions."*

Virtues and Choices

As we observe and consult about managing our money, we realize that our virtues and values influence our choices and affect how well our relationship thrives. When money is used in beneficial ways, it's a source of great good. As a couple and family, we can learn how to practice generosity, carry out responsibilities, distinguish between needs and wants, and manage financial activities effectively.

Choice and the use of Moderation are consistent themes as we consult about the topic of money. We can choose to be thrifty in managing our money, or we can spend lavishly. We consider charitable donations and how generously we give. When would giving a lot of money harm our family's well-being, and do we need to apply Moderation? We think about whether it's important to us to accumulate wealth and possessions. We assess whether we display competitive behavior, buying what we see others buying—the newest and best clothes, jewelry, videogame, vehicle, or home. What if we tried to keep up with this activity to the point that we went into debt?

Sharing from Experience: *"With our finances, we manage different aspects of the responsibility, but each of us sees the money that comes in and goes out." We also made a pact that we would not purchase a major household item unless we both especially liked it, so we protect our unity. That meant it took a* *long time to replace our bedspread, but we both had to like it. If one person did not find a choice attractive, there was no pleading or bargaining, we just kept looking, showing, and consulting.*

"We looked for a year for a bookcase, and we still couldn't find the right one. Then, one day, I saw a wonderful bookcase in the window of a furniture store. It was perfect for the space and quite handsome. I called my partner and requested that they go into this store and look at it. They came home later that day and said, 'Honey, did you really like that bookcase?'. I responded with 'Yes, I did!'. They happily said, 'Good, because I bought it!'. We are pleased to say that this happens to us often. If we are patient, we can find something we both like."

Effectively managing money relies significantly on the virtue of Dependability. It's an essential virtue when we have responsibilities, such as paying the family bills or taxes on time or managing a family member's funds. In these cases, we have confidence in each other to manage and account for money carefully. We maintain our Trust in each other because we demonstrate financial Dependability.

Additional virtues to consider are Justice and Respect. Neither of us should feel like we are begging the other for money. It's also not a weapon to use against each other. Both of us are full and equal partners with valuable roles. Even if one of us earns more money than the other, and even if one of us is a stay-at-home parent and doesn't contribute income to the relationship and family, we remain equal partners. It's fair for us to operate as a team when making financial decisions and setting guidelines for managing our money.

Future Planning

Another significant area of money management is our future. Many aspects of life will benefit from having savings and engaging in tax and estate planning, rather than just spending.

Below are some examples:

- Vacations
- Buying a home
- Education
- Retirement
- Potential illness
- Caregiving help for us or our relatives

Managing money often requires sacrifices. We may sacrifice for our children to benefit from an experience, or we may sacrifice spending in the present to build for the future. Regular consultation balances the needs of everyone in the family.

Sharing from Experience: *"Our marriage is a second one for both of us, so we came in with expectations of how we each liked to handle money. Early in our marriage, we held regular 'Economic Summits' where we consulted and determined what we needed as a couple and as individuals. Over time, these consultations have led us to establish a separate savings account for vacations. As circumstances change, we adjust what each of us contributes to our joint account. When we can accomplish our plans for our house and family, it's very satisfying and brings us closer together as a couple."*

The degree of harmony we achieve in our couple consultations about money indicates whether money is a connecting item or a source of conflict for us:

"The security and synergy of a committed financial partnership actually contributes to long-term financial success. Studies show that married people who behave as true financial partners tend to do better financially. Sure, you can find exceptions, but overall, having a strong commitment foundation increases the likelihood that you'll preserve your bond through the ups and downs on life's emotional roller-coaster and that you'll be financially secure. So although you take a risk when you tie your financial life to another in marriage, full financial partnership has benefits."[80]
Natalie H. Jenkins, Scott M. Stanley, William C. Bailey, and Howard J. Markman

When we have significant financial decisions to make or complex management issues to address, we make wiser choices by consulting with an expert third party. At times, we may also include others in consultations who would be affected by our decision. Expanding our consultations with input from others results in sound decisions that work for all of us. If we experience disunity, we can take a break and resume later. We apply Perseverance over time until we arrive at solutions.

Examples:

- "We will pay our bills on time or make responsible arrangements for payments."
- "As each of our children is born, we will establish an education fund for them."

- "We will give ____% of our income to charities."
- "We will invest ____% of income for our future retirement."
- "We will save a portion of every amount we earn."

Applying Virtues:

Below are some practical ways to incorporate virtues into daily practices with the theme of this chapter.

Orderliness
- Organize files and records for efficient retrieval and for use by those who need access.
- Seek professional help with money management as needed.
- Carry out bookkeeping tasks, being responsible for managing records to ensure accurate bill paying, banking, investing, tax reporting, and other financial transactions.

Self-Discipline
- Resist temptations to spend money outside the agreed plan we created based on our shared values.
- Avoid arguments about money that harm our relationship; instead, focus on consulting together to find shared agreements.
- Utilize personal strengths and skills to achieve prosperity.

Trust
- Share honestly what we value most about money and how it's used.
- Avoid manipulating or subverting each other's true intentions with money.

- Communicate openly and regularly about personal financial history, income, debts, spending, passwords, and all money management topics. [*Caution:* This should be paced with the stage of the relationship.]

Learning Activities:

1. Individually, write down our top three personal values related to money. Share and consult about them together. Next, determine the top three values related to money we will hold as a couple going forward.

2. Consult and compile a list of the value statements that will contribute to our making harmonious money-related decisions.

   Examples of value statements:

   - "Our children's education is a vital investment."
   - "Being careful with spending will conserve our resources."
   - "If possible, we will provide financial support to family members in need without requiring repayment."
   - "We will manage our finances with honesty and integrity."
   - "We will plan for our retirement."
   - "We will pay off all our debts before taking a major vacation."
   - "We will contribute to charities as part of our community outreach."

3. Reflect and consult about the following topics over an agreed spread of time, where they apply to us:

a. Who earns what and in what ways; How is money handled if there's only one income, or one partner has an income that's higher than the other one has
b. How much each can spend without consulting with the other partner first
c. How to pay the bills and who is responsible; How to save or invest funds; How to prepare for taxes
d. How much debt and risk are comfortable for each of us
e. Whether bank and investment accounts are separate, joint, or both
f. Whose name is shown as the owner of large items, such as vehicles and property
g. How or whether to budget; How much to donate to charities
h. How both are kept informed about the state of the finances
i. What is wasteful, generous, moderate, thrifty, or stingy
j. Who to loan money to or not loan to; who to borrow from or not borrow from
k. What insurance policies are necessary for us
l. What provisions are essential to have in our wills and included in estate planning
m. What professionals are needed to support financial decisions and activities

4. Meet with a financial planner or certified financial educator/counselor to ensure we are organized and effectively plan for our short- and long-term financial well-being, as well as that of our family. If we cannot afford a professional, then we should determine whether a family member or a friend could provide input or assistance instead. Both may also be useful.

5. Annually review our credit and borrowing capacity, any retirement funds we may have or expect to have, our wills and estate plans, and the status of any long-term debts, such as a home mortgage or vehicle loan. Update any related documents or plans.

6. Assess whether our ability to earn or manage money is being affected by societal systems or institutions that are unjust or prejudiced and interfering with our ability to progress (examples: access to loans, bank availability, hiring difficulties...). Create a plan that aligns with our virtue strengths and values, outlining how to address the identified issues and involving others as necessary.

Couple Reflection and Consultation:

Throughout this couple guide, there are invitations to practice the virtue of Reflection about your interactions and connection. This practice gives you opportunities to celebrate progress and consult to address issues.

1. What preparations and circumstances contribute to harmonious financial consultations between us?
2. What various emotions arise for us when we think about money?
3. What significant experiences from our pasts, individually and together, including those from our childhood and adolescence, shape our current financial attitudes and choices? Which ones are still useful for us to keep in mind now? Is it wise to challenge or change any of our views and approaches that are based on the past?
4. What values related to money do we have in common? Which ones are different? How can we manage our different values?

5. What are our top priorities for saving money? How much do we value saving and spending money on our children's education? To leave for relatives or charities upon our deaths?
6. What motivates us to earn an income? What new efforts, if any, do we want to make in how we generate income?
7. What legal contracts do we have that affect our finances?
8. What guidelines are useful for us related to spending money?
9. What motivates us when giving money to charity? What guidelines do we use when choosing charities to donate to?
10. What are our attitudes about borrowing: from family members, from friends, by going into debt with credit cards, or through obtaining a loan from a financial institution?
11. What is our status with debt? What is our plan for reducing it?
12. What is the status of our credit—the ability to borrow money for large expenditures? Do we need to improve our credit? How can we do this?
13. What is our attitude about loaning money to others? Under what circumstances might we choose to do this?
14. When do we use a budget? How strictly do we follow it? How do we handle situations where we are over budget?
15. What financial management systems and tools do we have confidence in and use?
16. What family relationship do we want to acknowledge through bequests in our wills? By naming them as beneficiaries on financial accounts or insurance?
17. Who could be dependable and help us with financial decisions and management?

Unifier 16: Growing from Difficulties

"See difficulties as learning opportunities that will expand your talents and capacities. Remind yourself that you can positively influence much of what happens in life."
Stephen Post

Focus Statement: Throughout our life together, we will face many difficulties, and we commit to navigating them as partners through consultation and growing individually and together in the process.

Deeper Learning:

We can prevent some difficulties or moderate the impact of others when we study and learn new information ahead of time. We see this in action in our lives as we learn about staying unified and as we practice connection activities.

However, the nature of life is that it has difficulties—the small, the challenging, and the devastating. They can arise from outside of our relationship, and they also happen between us. We have greater strength when we face problems together.

Learning Opportunities

When we notice learning opportunities during and after difficulties, we see that we can:

- Strengthen a virtue for a better response next time
- Benefit from asking for help and working as a team
- Deepen our communications
- Build our resilience

We can utilize challenging situations for growth when we respond to them positively and maturely. We can foster our physical, mental, emotional, and spiritual growth as individuals and as a couple.

"In exasperating situations, we must find the time to reflect if we are not afterwards to regret our words and actions. The Golden Rule, 'Do unto others what you would have them do unto you' or 'Do not do to others that which you do not wish done to yourself' is a useful guideline for action."[81] Mehri Sefidvash

When problems happen or we make mistakes, we can gain wisdom and practice good judgment. While "he" is used in this quotation below, the information applies to a partner as well:

"When faced with a problem, the spiritually immature person tries to escape. Instead of facing the problem, he hopes that someone else will resolve it or just go away. If he has committed an error, he blames another. If someone else commits an error, he attaches great importance to it and has a hard time forgiving. Instead of trying to find a solution to the problem, he concentrates on its cause, blaming persons or circumstances other than himself.

"In contrast, the spiritually mature person faces whatever problems arise with relative calm and decision. He recognizes and acknowledges whatever faults he may have committed which have contributed to the problem and accepts and forgives the errors made by others. He doesn't get bogged down in talking about who caused the problem or waste energy defending himself. He concentrates on searching for a good solution, using prayer for divine guidance, meditation, and consultation with

others. Then he willingly cooperates in carrying out the actions necessary to apply the solution."[82]
Joan B. Hernández

Here is further encouragement to eliminate a pattern of blame from your relationship:

"Making the effort to root out blame in your marital relationship is enormously worthwhile, and it is equally worthwhile to do this in your relationship with yourself! Blame is a cancer to be eradicated in every relationship you value, and it's critically important to develop a non-blameful relationship with yourself. Remember: Blame doesn't create growth. It is Empathy and Acceptance that are the two most powerful ingredients that help people grow and deal with problems. Remember this as you talk to yourself about your own behavior. Like anyone else who withers with blame and grows with empathy and acceptance, you need to create a climate of safety for yourself within which you can nurture your own growth."[83] Patty Howell and Ralph Jones

Unified Response to Difficulties

Every problem has unique aspects, and most will require specialized approaches. However, whatever the difficulty, we must apply our Unity to address it together as companions. Facing problems together as a couple assists us to:

- Share our thoughts and feelings
- Heal our wounds
- Address our fears
- Renew our love
- Strengthen our Trust

We improve our response to difficulties and unity when we use the virtue of Reflection and the communication skill of consultation. We use these approaches to give each other time to think and understand what is happening. Together, we devise practical solutions that neither of us would have come up with on our own. [See "Core Element B: Reflection and Consultation".]

Some problems are regular irritants that we must determine how to handle. For example, we know that fluctuating hormone levels can cause mood swings and physical symptoms, such as pain or the inability to function as well as we want. Variations like this in our well-being are continual opportunities to practice virtues such as Flexibility and Compassion.

Sharing from Experience: *"Every month, as my partner's hormones kicked in before her menstrual period, I became tense. She often became critical of things that she had previously easily ignored. She got angry and tearful. We both were very stressed about these experiences. It took some time and effort, but we searched for various solutions to make this time of the month easier for both of us, and we implemented some changes. It helped that we viewed this as something for us to address as a couple, rather than just a problem for her to handle on her own."*

However, many problems are more significant, and many of them involve aspects of loss and grief. Here are helpful ways to respond:

"Keep the channels of communication clear. Without an open and honest dialogue, a husband and wife will unknowingly build barriers around their hearts. They will journey separate paths and lose touch with one another. ...

Keeping communication channels open requires vulnerability. It demands your real feelings. It assumes your tears will roll down each other's cheeks."[84]
Les and Leslie Parrott

Sharing from Experience: *"We struggled in the early years of our marriage with not being able to have a child. Dealing with infertility often left us with sadness, frustration, and misunderstandings. Our relationship became increasingly focused on trying to have a child, rather than anything else. We recognized that we needed professional help and that we needed to refocus on our friendship and connection. Being reconnected made it possible for us to consult about new solutions. Today, we have two healthy children, and we are stronger together as a couple."*

Recovery Afterward

Recovery after a difficulty takes different lengths of time, depending on the severity of the challenge we experienced and the maturity of our skills. More minor daily issues don't take much time for us to work through. However, for more serious difficulties:

"Good marriages that have bumped into bad things do not recover quickly. Not generally, anyway. And smart couples do not buy into instant success plans that promise hurried ways to heal hearts or rapid roads to renewed relationships. They know better and, instead, expect slow progress, steadily building one marriage accomplishment upon another, like a game that is won one play at a time, or a building that is built brick by brick."[85]
Les and Leslie Parrott

When we know we have had a difficulty that will take time to recover from, we do our best to apply Compassion and Flexibility with each other. We may not be thinking as clearly as usual because of stress, so we try healing solutions and review how they work. We can then adjust and try new approaches and behaviors.

Sharing from Experience: *"One of the thorniest problems for us to consult through has been infidelity, and our issues were charged and intense. A professional therapist also assisted us; we could not have succeeded without their help. During and after therapy, we had to face each other and figure out a way to utilize consultation to maintain unity in our marriage. We needed a big space for consulting, and so we did most of it on walks outside. This gave each of us the chance to say what we needed to say. We had the space and distance to process our feelings and consider our options and responses without having to immediately speak.*

"As we walked, we were mindful of each other's emotional needs and state. Each of us had permission to say that we needed time to process our feelings and were not in a space to listen. Each of us had permission to speak only when we knew the other person was fully present in the moment. We wanted each other to be receptive to utilizing whatever comments came forth to keep our marriage together. When we began sharing or listening, if our feelings changed, we let the other person know.

"Once we decided to try to work through the infidelity and rebuild our marriage, each of us acted fully toward that end. We demonstrated Respect for each person's needs, including giving them time to process and understand what the other said. Sometimes, this required time alone or bringing up the same point in a slightly different way several times to gain understanding. Sometimes, it meant releasing resentment,

fear, and sorrow, and we gave the space to be sad. We needed time and space for each of us to process our feelings, to grieve, and to forgive. While consultation is used to 'solve' something, it's also a vehicle to get to truth. We use it to discover our own personal truths by sharing our thoughts and feelings and remaining open to one another's insights."

Life Is a Learning Experience

As we encounter difficulties and work through them together, we come to realize that life is a learning-in-action process. This realization makes it easier to relax and not try so hard to be perfect. We can bravely step forward to try something new with less worry about failure or criticism from each other or from other people. It's also easier to accept a mistake if we learn from it.

If we focus as individuals on strengthening our virtues in response to challenges, we will achieve victories and growth. As we navigate difficulties, our self-confidence grows, and we develop a mental toughness that can propel us through the next challenge that comes our way. We learn what we can do, and this spreads to all areas of our lives.

We strive to have the following be our attitude:

"See difficulties as learning opportunities that will expand your talents and capacities. Remind yourself that you can positively influence much of what happens in life. See yourself as capable and as an active participant in your world. Even when a problem has aspects that cannot be changed, trust that if you are resourceful, you will be able to use the situation to learn new ways of responding to it. Welcome change and challenge. Have faith that greater life meaning and satisfaction will emerge from each stressful situation."[86] Stephen Post

Even when we know the best ways to behave to maintain our relationship, we are still likely to struggle to carry them out at times. Our goal as human beings is always to demonstrate Excellence, but perfection isn't possible. Failures, which happen to everyone, strengthen our Humility and Trust in our ability to resolve the issues and rebound. [See "Unifier 17: Resolving and Rebounding".]

Difficulties offer opportunities to seek help, make amends, and learn new behaviors. Problems provide us with chances to strengthen our virtues and make better choices moving forward. Addressing issues instead of avoiding them increases the likelihood of nurturing a stronger, happier relationship as a couple.

Examples:

- "I'm angry and devastated that my job has ended."
- "Moving to be near our families is raising many issues from my childhood."
- "Our bank balance is getting very low. What will we do?"
- "The doctor says the lump is cancerous."
- "I'm dependent on drinking alcohol every day."
- "The car has a flat tire, and the spare tire is missing."

Applying Virtues:

Below are some practical ways to incorporate virtues into daily practices with the theme of this chapter.

Compassion
- Listen carefully to what each other shares about experiences and responses to difficulties.
- Offer comforting and supportive words.

- Reach out and offer assistance, and then wait to hear from our partner what is truly helpful.

Flexibility
- Adjust to a "new normal" when circumstances change.
- Make new plans when the original ones cannot happen.
- Hold ourselves still and quiet, rather than rushing into a response.

Humility
- Acknowledge that some happenings in life are difficult and not our preference.
- Respond when our help is needed and carry out tasks that we are not used to doing.
- Accept our limitations and recognize that we sometimes approach tasks and problems differently.

Learning Activities:

1. Identify a problem from the past and assess the learning or skill development that resulted from it. Identify a current problem that could benefit from what you have learned and apply the relevant solution.

2. Evaluate the impact of hormones on our bodily functions and emotional responses. Select two actions to address or improve our health and reactions.

3. Plan and carry out a trip, anticipating and preparing for potential difficulties. When difficulties arise, consult and work together to face them. After the trip, reflect on whether we were able to apply Flexibility and Unity. What did we learn from the experience?

4. Choose a home project to work on together. Set a target completion date and agreed-upon action steps to achieve it. Carry the project out. Reflect and consult with each other throughout to determine the next steps. What went well? Were we able to cooperate in unity? What were the difficulties? How did we handle them?

5. Evaluate a current difficult situation. What virtues could we apply to improve it? What lessons can be learned from it?

Couple Reflection and Consultation:

Throughout this couple guide, there are invitations to practice the virtue of Reflection about your interactions and connection. This practice gives you opportunities to celebrate progress and consult to address issues.

1. How do we generally respond to difficulties that arise?
2. If we spend time together dealing with a problem or emergency, does this bring us closer together? Why or why not?
3. What supports us in staying connected and responding as a united couple to a difficulty?
4. What have we learned from past difficulties? When have we successfully used learning from a difficult situation in new circumstances?
5. When has denial or temporary avoidance allowed us to gather our inner resources to cope with a difficulty? When does avoidance become unhealthy? (examples: turning to alcohol, drugs, shopping, sex...) In what ways are these or other actions enabling us to ignore what happened or is currently happening?

6. What do we want to improve about our responses to difficulties?
7. What virtues have we used well in difficult situations?
8. What specific virtues have we strengthened from working through a difficulty?
9. What virtues have we discovered are weaker as we respond to difficulties? How can we strengthen them to be more effective in the face of the next challenge?
10. When have we found it beneficial for our relationship to turn to professionals for help managing a difficulty? What was the outcome?
11. When have we successfully reached out and found help from others, such as family or friends, or accepted offered help when a problem was happening?
12. What is needed now in our life to address issues?

Unifier 17: Resolving and Rebounding

"Being kind and generous as well as granting pardon will
put you back on the same footing and keep your love strong."
H. J. Markman, S. M. Stanley, S. L. Blumberg,
N. H. Jenkins, and C. Whiteley

Focus Statement: We actively resolve issues and forgive with our minds and hearts, maintaining unity and resiliently thriving together.

Deeper Learning:

It's wise to keep our lives as "cleaned up" as possible, regardless of the size of the issue. However, we recognize that minor issues are easier to address promptly, and more significant ones may require time to resolve.

When we truly address, repair, and resolve issues, they don't keep coming back up and disrupting our relationship. When we choose to forgive and let go of hurt feelings, we create a space for unity to reappear and disunity to dissipate. Resolving issues, especially big ones, includes being effective at:

- Reflecting and consulting to understand what happened and why, including identifying whether there was a vital need not being met
- Applying our Humility and acknowledging our errors; taking responsibility for words or actions that caused hurt feelings or problems
- Regretting our parts in what happened; repenting
- Cleaning up whatever problems we have caused or are partially responsible for
- Asking each other for forgiveness

- Truly granting pardon so that our minds and hearts are calm, and we put the issue in the past
- Learning from what occurred and from the clean-up process
- Applying the learning to demonstrate improved behaviors
- Demonstrating Respect for ourselves and acknowledging our efforts to grow
- Being resilient in continuing with our relationship in a healthy way

The longer we stay stuck in our poor choice and its consequences, the deeper the hole we dig. We become emotionally and mentally stuck in the past. This influences our present, future, and often our involvement in many aspects of life. Progress takes courage. Making an effort to resolve what happened and moving forward resiliently empowers us to have a better present and future. We are lighter and happier when we are not dragging unresolved issues along with us.

Forgiveness

Forgiveness is crucial in resolving issues, although it's often tough to do. Counselor and marriage educator Michele Weiner-Davis is very direct with couples about why it's so important:

"Don't pretend that you are putting effort into your marriage when you have a mental ledger book detailing your spouse's every wrongdoing. As long as you are holding on to resentments of the past, you can't be forgiving. As long as you are not forgiving, you can't be loving. As long as you aren't loving, you can't do what it takes to make your marriage work. So decide. Are you going to carry a grudge and stand by while you and your spouse become a divorce statistic or are you going to rid yourself of the shackles of the past which have held you prisoner? Forgive your spouse and start anew."[87] Michele Weiner-Davis

We can describe forgiveness in many ways. Some of these are:

- Pardoning someone for saying or doing something hurtful or harmful
- Giving up a desire for revenge
- Letting go of anger and resentment

Bravely requesting and offering forgiveness to each other strengthens our Respect and Unity. We notice that our missteps become learning opportunities, which then inform actions that benefit us and others. It can be powerful for us to look back at something that has transformed since we failed or caused harm. [See "Unifier 16: Growing from Difficulties".]

If our words or actions harm each other or others, we may feel that we cannot ask for forgiveness, or the issue may not feel complete until we clean up the problems we caused. We can usually take concrete actions to resolve issues arising from our behavior. However, we must ensure that any remedial actions we consider will not cause further harm, including to ourselves. We demonstrate Respect and maintain our dignity while addressing the situation.

We may find these five ways of carrying out a forgiveness process useful, as suggested by the authors of *When Sorry Isn't Enough*:

1. Expressing Regret: "I am sorry."
2. Accepting Responsibility: "I was wrong."
3. Making Restitution: "What can I do to make it right?"

4. Genuinely Repenting: "I want to change."
5. Requesting Forgiveness: "Can you find it in your heart to forgive me?"

The authors suggest that many factors are important to consider when offering an apology. These are summarized below.

- Our tone of voice and body language must match our words for the receiver to believe that our apology is sincere.
- State specifically what the apology is for and acknowledge the hurt that has been caused.
- Avoid using language such as "…but…" that conveys blame to the person we are apologizing to; attacks or defensiveness rarely lead to forgiveness and reconciliation.
- Don't use an apology to try to manipulate someone; for example, apologize in the hope that the recipient will change some behavior.
- Depending on the circumstances and relationship, we may find it most effective to put our apology in writing.[88]
Summarized from Gary Chapman and Jennifer Thomas

Forgiveness isn't the same as ignoring the situation or saying that what happened was okay. The initial problem still needs to be addressed—just as we are responsible for our own actions, so are others responsible for theirs. The next step, then, of course, is for us to be clear about what behaviors to improve and begin to address them. This fuels our resilience and recovery.

Sharing from Experience: *"We both love to be helpful to each other. However, we have learned that it's wise and* demonstrates Respect to consult with each other before jumping in with unasked-for assistance. One incident made this understanding clear to us.

"We were both working in the yard in different places. I climbed the ladder with an electric trimmer and began cutting off branches from a tree. I let them fall to the ground. My partner saw what I was doing, came over, and began gathering up the fallen branches and clearing the area around the base of the ladder.

"Unfortunately, they bumped their shoulder against the ladder, distracting me and making me feel unsafe. As I moved in response, I cut the electrical cord attached to the trimmer. This tripped the power off to our whole home, and I came close to falling from the ladder. I yelled, 'You could have waited to clean up until after I was done!'. I was angry and upset.

"Later that day, after we calmed down and we were able to talk about the situation, my partner said, 'I'm sorry for getting in the way and causing the accident.' I responded with, 'I forgive you. And...I'm sorry I yelled at you.'

"We consulted about what happened and how to prevent a similar incident from happening again. We realized we had skipped consulting with each other about responsibilities before going outside to work. I was also able to share that it would have worked better for me if we had consulted briefly about the timing of the help before it started."

Forgiveness frees us from holding a grudge against someone for what they did. Forgiveness is choosing to reject "vengeance, renounce bitterness, break the silence of estrangement, and actually wish the best" for the other person.[89] (Les and Leslie Parrott) It takes courage for us to ask for forgiveness and apply our Compassion to grant it, especially when what seemed to have happened felt unfair. It takes courage to address the issues so we can re-establish fairness and unity. It takes both our minds and our hearts to accomplish the task.

Courage and love are interlinked:

"Courage is love as action—love on her silver steed, forcing change in the world, rising to challenges, negotiating life with skill, and confronting others with care and wisdom. The qualities that courage draws upon—hardiness and resilience, as well as the ability to bend and alter course when faced with difficulty, to commit oneself to a cause, and to find inner power during times of pain—are *all* associated with mental health. We need a deep, tensile strength to face the tough times in life, to speak out persuasively against injustice, and, above all, to love others wisely and well. To love at all is a risk that requires courage—we risk our safety, letting ourselves be raw and vulnerable; we accept our share of compromise and weather disappointment and despair; and above all, we are willing to confront a loved one even if what we need to say is not easy or kind."[90] Stephen Post

This perspective addresses applying both our minds and our hearts:

"When you forgive, you need to do more than say the words and mean them. You also have to extend a forgiving, helping hand. To truly forgive, you need to be gracious to your partner. Being kind and generous as well as granting pardon will put you back on the same footing and keep your love strong."[91] Howard J. Markman, Scott M. Stanley, Susan L. Blumberg, Natalie H. Jenkins, and Carol Whiteley

Forgiveness needs to be sincere and honest. It's not wise to forgive someone automatically because the situation is difficult or because we feel unhappy that the other person is regretful. The problem will not be easily resolved if we claim to forgive someone while still harboring considerable anger, sadness, or pain from the incident. Some inner healing likely needs to happen first.

Once a problem is resolved, it's wise for us to leave it in the past and not bring it up again. Reminding someone about the situation can indicate that we did not completely forgive the first time, and we interfere with rebounding and rebuilding. Of course, we are also engaged in the necessary behavioral adjustments and making amends, so similar situations occur less frequently and eventually stop happening.

Caution: When there are serious issues between you, such as infidelity, or there are repeated and serious misbehaviors, mental illnesses, or crimes, please seek professional assistance and/or help from civil authorities.

Bouncing Back Resiliently

When we experience a difficulty between us or from some other cause or direction in life, we know it's in our best interest to handle it well and bounce back afterward. The efforts we make with resilience move us toward feeling love and unity in the face of the situation. Here is a perspective on resilient people. They:

"... have three distinguishing characteristics: an acceptance of reality, a strongly held belief that life is meaningful, and an ability to find creative solutions to seemingly insoluble problems."[92] Janet A. Khan

We see that we are effective in applying resilience when we:

- Stay engaged, optimistic, and aware when faced with difficult events or experiences
- Accept and adapt to change, stressful circumstances, and difficult events, drawing on resourcefulness and inner strength
- Act calmly during crises and take positive steps to manage them
- Seek creative, effective, and appropriate solutions to difficult problems
- Process, grieve, and recover from failures, disruptive events, losses, and disappointments, seeking help to heal, learn, grow, and recover as needed
- Feel motivated to recover due to a belief that life is meaningful
- Learn from challenges how to prevent them from recurring or to improve responses in the future
- Mature from experiences, discovering new capabilities and strengths
- Carry on steadfastly even after responding to and grieving from emotional blows
- Continue moving forward in life in positive ways after difficulties[93] Marriage Transformation

We often need to accompany and encourage one another to be resilient. On our own, we can become stuck in an issue for longer than necessary or wise.

When we value our unity and decrease our tolerance for disunity, it motivates us to seek resolution. We address issues as needed so they don't linger and harm our relationship. Our commitment to unity enables us to be thorough in our forgiveness process. Our focused attention on healing positions us to bounce back resiliently.

Examples:

- "I know my anger at my mother's behavior keeps coming out as attacks on you—I agree to go to counseling sessions to address this—please forgive me for hurting you."
- "I wasn't paying enough attention when I was cleaning the garage, and I threw away something important to you—I'm very sorry for doing that. Please forgive me. [Wait for a response before offering how to address it.] I know it will not be the same, but may I buy a new one for you?"
- "I forgot to pick up your medicine from the store when I drove past—I apologize, and I will go back immediately."
- Our current method of handling bills isn't working for me. We keep getting behind on paying them, and I get angry every time. Can we please consult about a new approach?"

Applying Virtues:

Below are some practical ways to incorporate virtues into daily practices with the theme of this chapter.

Compassion
- See beyond the immediate actions our partner took; look at the whole person, consider the context of their life circumstances, and hold a spirit of goodwill, recognizing that our partner did not intend to cause the harm that occurred.

- Acknowledge the inner pain each feels and behave gently and kindly to begin healing.
- Release attachment to what happened, and open ourselves consciously to reconnect in a loving way.

Perseverance
- Recognize when forgiveness is a process that will take time, and stay engaged for as long as is needed to carry out all possible actions to clean up the situation and bring it to completion.
- Continue to make efforts to improve communication and behavior.
- Identify and carry out actions to resiliently rebound.

Unity
- See the bigger picture of the whole relationship and value it rather than holding onto resentment or grudges and building walls between us.
- Consciously observe the thoughts and emotions that are in the way of reuniting, acknowledge them, and do our best to let them go.
- Address any areas where we need to apply Justice, consulting together to determine new behaviors that are fair to both of us and will lead to resiliency and harmony.

Learning Activities:

1. Identify an issue that's still somewhat unresolved, identify remediation actions to take that will not likely cause harm, and take concrete steps toward forgiveness and healing. Consult and reflect on the situation and outcome, capturing any lessons learned, and determining what can prevent such an occurrence from happening again.

2. Create a healing ceremony for moving forward after an issue. Examples of elements that could be included are music, prayer, dancing or other movements, writing down issues or concerns and burning them, using water to cleanse our hands or bodies, and so on.

3. Identify a past incident and the lessons learned from it. Consult and agree on how our learning can, in turn, contribute to other people. Take at least one action step to apply the learning to benefit another person. If one of our lessons learned is already contributing to other people, celebrate the contributions already underway.

4. Identify an issue that has been forgiven, but we are not as reconnected as we want to be. Take two concrete action steps to feel closer together.

Couple Reflection and Consultation:

Throughout this couple guide, there are invitations to practice the virtue of Reflection about your interactions and connection. This practice gives you opportunities to celebrate progress and consult to address issues.

1. What supports us in effectively coping during times of stress when one of us unintentionally does something hurtful to the other?
2. Why is it essential that forgiveness comes from both our minds and our hearts?
3. When we are tempted to raise a previously settled issue, what can prevent us from doing so? When might it be important to refer to a previous issue instead?
4. How can being committed to unity between us facilitate our ability to offer forgiveness and agree to forgive?

5. If it feels like there's pressure to forgive before we are ready, how does this affect us and the situation? What virtues can we apply to make waiting easier?
6. When might humor be appropriate and positive, so we handle difficult situations more lightly?
7. How can practicing gratitude for our blessings contribute to our well-being and resolving issues?
8. In what ways does sincerely practicing Service for one another make the process of forgiveness and rebounding go more smoothly?
9. What are a few practical ways we can use to reconnect after something harmful has happened, and we have addressed it?
10. What approaches increase our resilience after we have resolved an issue?
11. Are there any current issues for us to address and resolve? Given all we just learned, what is our best approach to it now?

Section 6:

Expanding Beyond Us

Section 6 Introduction

As a couple, you interact with a larger circle of people. Some you see only occasionally, but others you're with daily. The strength of your union enables you to maintain constructive relationships with them.

From the foundation of unity, commitment, and cooperation you're building, you become a rich resource and example to your family, friends, and community. Your children thrive on the security of knowing you're deeply connected and love one another. Your family becomes one of many that provides a solid foundation for society.

You nurture friendships that enrich your lives, and you maintain a home that you're happy inviting people into. You offer the gifts of your Compassion and caring to those in your community. You have the well-being and strength to contribute to the lives of others.

Here in Section 6, you will expand your couple circle of unity to include other people:

- Unifier 18: Establishing Family Harmony
- Unifier 19: Connecting with Friends and Community

Unifier 18: Establishing Family Harmony

*"At the center of...expanding concentric circles of unity
is the family, and the foundation of the family is the
relationship between the wife and husband."*
Raymond and Furugh Switzer

Focus Statement: We value growing our unity and operating harmoniously in our family relationships, demonstrating Respect and love to those connected to us, spending quality time with them, and treating them with kindness and care.

Deeper Learning:

We highly value our relationship and consider our unity and connection vital for our well-being and survival. Adding children expands our circle of unity, and we become a family. However, we remember that the quality of our relationship is the stable foundation for the family, so we pay attention to maintaining it. William J. Doherty, a psychologist, shares his perspectives:

"Adjustments [to having a child] ... are natural and inevitable. But there is a difference between adjusting your marriage to meet your children's needs and losing your marriage to parenthood."[94] "Children are natural and eager consumers of whatever time, attention, and goods and services that parents will provide. It's the job of parents to discern how much is enough, how much is too much, and to enforce the difference."[95] "The greater danger for most of us is to lose our marriage to the demands of parenthood rather than losing our kids to the demands of our marriage (although this happens sometimes in stepfamilies). In a two-parent family, we

236

either fight to create and keep a marriage-centered family, in which the couple relationship is the stable fulcrum of the family and the couple together care for their children, or we become a child-centered family in which the marriage goes on the shelf."[96]

As our family becomes more complex, the challenges we face in maintaining unity also increase, a topic that will be explored later in this chapter. [More about family unity is also in "Core Element A: Commitment to Unity".]

Being Unified As a Couple and As Parents

We strive to consult and agree on how we parent, creating a positive, healthy, and well-functioning family. This includes sibling relationships that are loving, unified, and supportive. We study how to parent effectively and learn from experienced individuals how to provide discipline, education, and engaging activities. We also reach out for help as needed.

Sharing from Experience: *"In the weeks following our daughter's birth, we felt like we were moving through a fog of exhaustion. Other than an occasional hug, we barely felt like a couple. Then, one morning, after a few hours of sleep, we realized we had missed each other! We consulted with my mother, who lived nearby. She agreed to come over after the baby was asleep and stay there for an hour. We only went to a local restaurant for dessert, but that was enough to remind us that we had non-baby things to talk about and our friendship and relationship to maintain.*

"We committed to go out on a date every few weeks, and we have kept it up through the arrival of a second child and several years of parenting. It was one of the best decisions we ever made. Our children are happier when they see us happy

together. They know we are united, so they don't try to get one of us to make a decision without agreement from the other. We see them thriving in school and with friendships, in part because they know their home situation is healthy and stable."

Parenting isn't easy, but we view it as a vitally important responsibility that we carry out together. As our children grow, we strive to guide them in making positive choices. We want them to have meaningful and purposeful lives that incorporate virtues and service, navigate hardship effectively, practice self-discipline and accountability, and engage in the arts and sciences as they excel in their education.

Constructive Discipline

How to guide and discipline our children is a regular topic of consultation for us. We encounter many opinions on the topic from various sources, which can sometimes be confusing. We also struggle to agree on our approach at times. Overall, however, we see discipline as a form of teaching, not punishment:

"The goal of effective parental authority is to enable children to develop their own inner authority, a sense of personal responsibility, and an ability to make conscious moral choices. The younger children are, the more dependent they are on a fair and loving parent to guide and discipline their behavior. Clear, reasonable discipline gives children the foundation for self-discipline. … The patterns of behavior an educative parent focuses on are the virtues."[97] Linda Kavelin Popov

Being unified as parents means that we consult regularly with each other, try out new approaches, and sometimes defer to each other's ideas. It's not easy to be in harmony as parents, and it requires Perseverance.

Family Consultation

Our children often see us consulting with each other. As they have grown, we have gradually introduced them to consultation by offering simple choices for them to consider together, such as what they might want to wear or eat. When they reached about age 5, we introduced them to family consultation, keeping meetings at lengths that fit their capacities and attention spans. These family meetings are held regularly for a period of time and then sometimes become less frequent, but we continue to hold them as needed to ensure everyone has a voice in matters that affect some or all of us.

Family consultations provide every member with practice in making suggestions for topics, leading a meeting, speaking, listening, taking notes, making decisions, and planning. In her book, *Family Matters*, Monette Van Lith says children appreciate these elements about family meetings:

- "Provides a safe space to express their feelings
- Gives them a chance to have their voice heard and their ideas discussed
- Creates a sense of belonging and purpose
- Provides experiences of making progress together
- Involves everyone in planning for family activities."[98]

We have discovered that these family consultations are great opportunities to practice virtues. For example, if one of us is troubled and asks for help from the others, we can practice Compassion to assist each other with talking about and sorting out our thoughts and feelings. We can apply Creativity to come up with ways to offer support and solutions.

Of course, not every issue is suitable for the whole family to discuss. Some matters are best discussed privately.

Family coach Monette Van Lith, as quoted above, encourages making family meetings enjoyable by incorporating fun elements, such as snacks, art activities, age-appropriate games, or other engaging activities. We begin by celebrating achievements, and we share words of appreciation with one another throughout. We all feel happier and more secure when we are united and understand each other.

Someone Shares Their Experience: *"There are many everyday occurrences that often result in happiness, smiles, or laughter for me: hugging and cuddling with my partner, watching our children get along and help around the house, watching humorous videos, petting our cat, reading, telling jokes, cooking yummy food, listening to fun music together, tickling my kids, and visiting or chatting with friends and family."*

Our Extended Family

Beyond interacting with our children, we also recognize that our extended family provides many opportunities to practice Unity. These family members include our parents, grandparents, aunts, uncles, cousins, stepparents, step- or half-siblings, and more. In addition, many of them have extended family members that we see at times, such as at events like family reunions, weddings, and funerals.

Growing family unity with everyone can be energizing and wonderful. Spending time together can include special experiences and create wonderful memories. We often seek wisdom and support from family members. It can also feel challenging at times as everyone tries to get along.

We feel happier and emotionally secure when we have positive relationships with our extended family members. We strive to be harmonious with them and demonstrate Service whenever possible and when it's healthy. We also know when to set boundaries so that interactions show Respect.

One aspect of interacting with family members is that it becomes easy to see each other's faults and failings when we are so close. It's more constructive to see each other's virtues and good actions. Shifting to appreciate the positive in each person can improve our attitude toward them, if needed. [See "Unifier 8: Appreciating One Another".]

Despite all our best efforts, there are times when interactions are challenging, and we must consult to find solutions. When extended family members get angry or criticize us, we may want to avoid them. We can comfort and support each other, but it's wise to avoid criticizing family members, as we may take it personally. We find better solutions when we use our Compassion to seek understanding and Creativity to find positive ways to calm our reactions.

Beyond our natural difficulties in getting along with family members at times, there may be indicators of more significant problems. In very difficult or abusive circumstances, it's only possible to contribute to family unity when there's no contact, and we send positive thoughts or say prayers for the troubled person. We can then maintain some hope that the circumstances will improve. If we experience some degree of absent, neglectful, mentally ill, addicted, arguing, abusive, or even violent family members, we may struggle with pain from the circumstances. We may be wise to seek professional assistance to guide us in learning how to respond constructively. We contact mental health professionals or seek legal help with serious problems.

As we consult about our extended family relationships and how to increase unity with each person as suitable, we recognize that our goal is to be a healthy family. Virginia Satir sees the following patterns in what she calls "vital and nurturing families":

- "Self-worth is high.
- Communication is direct, clear, specific, and honest.
- Rules are flexible, human, appropriate, and subject to change.
- The link to society is open and hopeful and is based on choice."

She further states, "The changes all rest on new learnings, new awareness and a new consciousness. Everyone can achieve these."[99]

Complexity of Stepfamilies

Stepfamilies have their own dynamics, and we have experienced elements of them. Sometimes, it's possible to establish close and loving relationships, while at other times, it's a struggle. According to Maggie Scarf, author of *Remarriage Blueprint*, the "insider/outsider" forces are powerful. They often challenge our ideal of family unity. We see children in the family confused about who to love or be loyal to, and they sometimes struggle to feel secure. Issues such as discipline, money, time, family celebrations, and more are complex. It's great that so many resources are available for all our family circumstances. Author Ron Deal has provided some of them, and he says:

> "Take your blindfold off and learn what a healthy blended family is and does, and the odds of your success increase dramatically. When you know how to be a smart stepfamily, integration, or the merging of your two

families, is accelerated and the rewards to both children and adults increase dramatically."[100] Ron Deal

As we strive to grow our unity with blended family members and everyone in our extended family, we consider and strive to carry out such behaviors as:

- Having a positive attitude
- Greeting one another pleasantly
- Demonstrating Respect for each other's living area and possessions
- Accepting each other's preferences
- Having meals with each other
- Reaching out consistently with positive communications
- Praying together
- Sharing activities
- Preserving family memorabilia
- Telling stories about positive family experiences
- Helping each other with tasks
- Acknowledging and celebrating positive progress

When we sincerely wish to have loving hearts toward people who are family, regardless of how loosely connected, we feel empowered to continue striving for unity.

A Larger Circle of Unity

We have begun to see that the unity in our couple relationship and harmony in our family provide part of the foundation for the broader unity of our community and the human family. This topic will be addressed further in the next chapter, "Unifier 19: Connecting with Friends and Community."

We can discover what it takes to stay united as we seek opportunities to interact harmoniously within our family—regardless of its strengths, composition, or challenges. This will enhance our ability to foster unity among people. Here is a broader view of the importance of marriage and family:

> "Humanity has developed through different stages of groupings: families, clans, tribes, villages, cities, nation states, and, now, the whole world. At the center of these expanding concentric circles of unity is the family, and the foundation of the family is the relationship between the wife and husband. Our understanding is that marriage holds within it the seed of the wider unity and is a significant working ground for this ultimate goal. From this perspective we can see how marriage functions not only for the best interests of both partners and their offspring, but that it also serves a higher, more expansive purpose...."[101] Raymond and Furugh Switzer

We aim to be a happy, unified family actively involved in education, work, and community service. Harmony, unity, well-being, and love are high ideals in human relationships, especially in a family, and it takes our focused effort to create them. Positive relationships within our home extend outward to include everyone we consider to be family members and beyond. Our ability to reach out and include others in our lives enriches us, and we all develop skills that grow unity.

Examples:

- Teach children a new skill.
- Have a regular meal with our extended family members.
- Share tasks related to caring for our older family members.

- Assist each other with home maintenance tasks.
- Hold regular family meetings.

Applying Virtues:

Below are some practical ways to incorporate virtues into daily practices with the theme of this chapter.

Dependability
- Make and keep promises and commitments that foster our ability to rely on one another.
- Handle responsibilities that keep our family moving in a positive direction.
- Set and maintain consistent learning and behavior standards for our children to strive for.

Flexibility
- Accept and adjust to each other's personality, using gentle humor as needed.
- Arrange times for family members to be together, even when it's challenging to coordinate.
- Adjust to life changes, such as illness, death, moving, or weddings that bring new family members, and respond effectively to their needs and unexpected events.

Service
- Consult with appropriate family members about the actions they consider helpful and their preferences for how our family and home operate.
- Carry out thoughtful actions for family members that align with their needs and preferences, learning to do new actions as needed.

- Express gratitude consistently for the words we use and the actions each of us carries out to benefit our family members and extended family relationships.

Learning Activities:

1. Create a family mission statement, with our children as appropriate, and display it where everyone in the family can see it. "A family mission statement is a combined, unified expression from all family members of what your family is all about—what it is you really want to do and be—and the principles you choose to govern your family life."[102] Stephen R. Covey

2. Write a list of what we appreciate about each of our children, parents, grandparents, siblings, and other close family members, focusing on those who are alive. If applicable, also write a list of what we appreciate, or appreciated in the past, about the relationship between us and these close family members.

3. Create a fun video of our family or a photo collection that represents our family life. Share what we created with family members.

4. Collect a few positive or quirky family stories that demonstrate our family's culture. Create a family gathering and share the stories, or share them at an occasion we attend.

5. Create and serve a meal for a few extended family members that includes some of their favorite foods. Involve them in the cooking if they wish.

6. Establish a pattern of holding family meetings, involving all those living in our home according to their capacities.

7. Work with our children to create drawings, letters, or greeting cards for older family members and deliver or send them.

8. Plan a celebration that includes elements of the ethnic culture(s) of one or more family members.

Couple Reflection and Consultation:

Throughout this couple guide, there are invitations to practice the virtue of Reflection about your interactions and connection. This practice gives you opportunities to celebrate progress and consult to address issues.

1. How do we describe our family? What do we acknowledge as our family virtues and strengths?
2. What virtues do we choose as guides for our immediate family? For our extended family?
3. What do we like about our relationships with our children?
4. What is working well in educating and encouraging our children to develop many virtue strengths? What do we want to improve? How will we accomplish that?
5. What does family unity mean to us? How can we foster greater family unity?
6. What do we appreciate about our relationships with extended family members?
7. What challenges do we face in our immediate family relationships? In our extended ones? How can we address or overcome the difficulties? What do we need to accept?

8. What gets in the way of our demonstrating Respect and courtesy to family members? How could we practice Unity in more of our interactions?
9. What boundaries are wise for us to establish to prevent harm from problematic family members?
10. What thoughtful actions can we offer to various family members? How will we carry them out?

Unifier 19: Connecting with Friends and Community

"Offering whatever we can in the spirit of sharing and service, and also of joint experience, is...part of hospitality."
Agnes Ghaznavi

Focus Statement: We are a strong and unified couple with vital connections with our friends, neighbors, and the community around us, and we actively spend time with them for our mutual well-being and enjoyment.

Deeper Learning:

Positive relationships with our friends and neighbors, individually and collectively as a couple or family, contribute to our overall happiness and well-being. Building those relationships often feels easy to do, and it's energizing. However, when we are focused on our responsibilities and activities, it can feel challenging to take the time to participate. Even when we are tired, though, we stay in action, as we recognize the necessity of striking a balance between managing our own lives and being part of the lives of others. This balance contributes to achieving harmony and fosters a thriving relationship.

As we reflect on what is important to us and consult about how to utilize our available time, we draw on Creativity to find ways to connect with others. We have mutual and individual friends who are supporters of our union, and we schedule time with them. We know many of our neighbors, and we strive to apply Politeness and Sociability when interacting with them in positive and friendly ways. As we reach out to neighbors and friends, it draws us together. We gain people to celebrate with and help us during difficulties. This network of people can also collaborate in building a better community around us.

Expanding Friendships

When we reflect on our life, we realize that sometimes our circle of people is too limited. Involvement with friends and people in a community can enrich our conversations, encourage our personal growth, and unite us when we participate together. We could join a book discussion, exercise club, spiritual gathering, community theater, sports team, game-playing gathering, or any other group that interests us. (*Possible resource to use:* https://www.meetup.com/.)

Developing new friendships or neighbor relationships that enrich our lives can take courage. We may encounter barriers at times, such as prejudices, distrust, a lack of financial resources, competition, comparison, fear of rejection, a shortage of time and energy, discomfort with the state of our home and environment, and more. How can we overcome barriers like these? What are the most important things to us? What virtues, personal growth, and couple practices can assist us with connecting with new people?

We also notice that it's beneficial for us to form friendships with other couples that we both like and enjoy. We can validate that some challenges are typical, and we can solve problems together while maintaining appropriate privacy. Finding couples who are a good match for us can be challenging, but it's worth the time investment, as we can have fun together and support each other in maintaining healthy relationships.

Hospitality

We began consulting about hospitality in "Unifier 11: Enjoying Social Time". When our relationship and family life feel harmonious and united, inviting others into our home can extend our happiness. We can relax, get to know others, share what is important to us, and enjoy developing meaningful friendships.

> "Sharing is part of hospitality, not only materially but also spiritually: the atmosphere, the qualities of the members of the household. Learning is another aspect: 'peeping in at the window' into another family's way of living is the privilege and benefit of the guests. Offering whatever we can in the spirit of sharing and service, and also of joint experience, is also part of hospitality. Hospitality in the home is a most important way of learning about the outside world. People bring into the home other customs, opinions and ways of doing things, and children as well as adults widen their horizons in increased understanding of the world of human beings."[103] Agnes Ghaznavi

As we develop true friendships and offer hospitality, conversations may naturally flow into discussing how to contribute to one another, our shared neighborhood, or the wider community.

The Wider Community

Community building and betterment are ways our unity as a couple can contribute to others. We reach out to neighbors, other parents, colleagues, and more to establish cooperative working relationships or true friendships. We view our relationships and families as the fundamental building blocks of our community. We learn that we can collaborate with diverse people and become friends with them in the process. When we spend time together, we can include meaningful conversations, fun social time and laughter, educational support for children and teens, creative activities that benefit our neighborhood or community, and more.

Community building that includes laughter could look like this:

> "Like a good roll of duct tape, humor bonds us to each other. It strengthens us as a community, and it allows us to transcend our differences and our barriers. ... Only when we can get past ourselves, when we can laugh past our perceived superiority and righteousness, can we truly look at our neighbor with a sense of hospitality and justice. ... We all laugh in the same language.... When we laugh together, we not only cross barriers, but we also bond together as community."[104] Susan Sparks

We know that practicing Service toward each other is a vital and healthy element of our relationship. [See "Unifier 13: Giving Thoughtful Service".] Looking outward then includes us choosing to demonstrate Service to others. Acting to better the community around us trains us to consult in groups, collaborate to accomplish tasks, and think selflessly about the needs of others. This great skill also applies in a family. We apply Respect in all circumstances, ensuring that everyone involved is included in consultations and is satisfied with the decisions and outcomes.

Engaging in practicing Service means that we move beyond our self-centered activities and concerns. When we serve people together, it can lift our minds, hearts, and souls to a higher level, and it can strengthen our relationship. However, we must remember to use Moderation, so we continue to meet the needs of our relationship, family, and home.

Sharing from Experience: *"When we began our relationship, we recognized that it was essential for us to engage in activities that benefited others and to observe how well we worked together. After exploring possible ideas, we determined that we were living in an area prone to frequent severe storms, but it lacked an adequate emergency plan. We observed that one of us is comfortable in a leadership position, while the other prefers to work behind the scenes; we valued both. It was extraordinarily satisfying for both of us to create a coalition of people from the government and the community and develop a response plan together.*

"Now that we are in a committed relationship, community service has become an integral part of who we are and what we do. It's a passion that energizes us and unites us with a shared purpose."

When we practice Humility and Respect during community service, we:

- Develop true friendships,
- Learn new perspectives from others, and
- Contribute meaningfully to the lives of others.

When we involve our children, they also gain new perspectives, build lasting skills, and strengthen many virtues, such as their virtue of Service. Being able to contribute to others rather than being self-centered has long-lasting implications:

"In essence, generativity is the act of preparing another's garden for spring. It's power in the service of love. It's an

253

act of giving that enables another person to manifest his or her own strengths and gifts through love. It can be as simple as listening and giving support to others—renewing their sense of self and hope. It can be as demanding as raising a child well, or mentoring a student in a difficult and challenging field.... [G]enerativity in *high school* predicts good physical and mental health in late adulthood, a time interval of over *fifty* years."[105] Stephen Post

If we feel uncertain about or even resistant to being involved in our community, we can think about this:

"It may seem as if individuals and families that are struggling to address their own needs in a disintegrating social order have no time for community building. Yet, it is precisely in the context of the community that they will find the means to solve their problems. ... When each member of the community seeks to address the well-being of the others, the powers of the community are multiplied and all receive blessings and assistance in a way that attending to one's own problems can never achieve."[106] Paul Lample

Sharing from Experience: *"Over the summer, while our children were out of school, we relocated to a more diverse neighborhood within the city, near a park and playground. Living closer to more people was an adjustment, but we soon discovered how easy it was to have conversations with others. We got involved at a community center that offered activities for children and teens. Soon, it became natural for us and the other parents to come together and address our mutual concerns."*

As we expand our own couple and family circle to include many other people, our lives become richer. We discover new opportunities to strengthen our virtues, and we lift our eyes away from our daily responsibilities. Each time we reach out, we learn we are connected to many people who care.

Examples:

- Facilitate a study session or an ongoing group to explore a meaningful or engaging topic.
- Host a consultation or prayer gathering focused on finding solutions for a community issue.
- Visit neighbors and friends in their homes or a neighborhood gathering place.
- Coordinate or participate in a community beautification or improvement project.
- Volunteer our time to support a worthy cause.
- Visit or volunteer at a care facility or help older people in their homes.
- Offer tutoring or classes for the intellectual, moral, or spiritual education of children or teens.
- Offer friendship, mentorship, and guidance to groups of pre-teens or teens.
- Join a committee addressing a civic or social issue.
- Encourage group participation in the arts, such as arranging a neighborhood concert or poetry reading.
- Volunteer at a museum, concert hall, theater, or library.
- Enjoy a once-a-month social time with friends.
- Organize and host a neighborhood picnic.
- Foster children.
- Set up a literacy program for adults.
- Host constructive consultations about social issues such as poverty, racism, or environmental concerns.

- Volunteer with a civic, arts, or healthcare organization.
- Participate in an annual food drive for those in need.

Applying Virtues:

Below are some practical ways to incorporate virtues into daily practices with the theme of this chapter.

Politeness and Sociability
- Reach out to create and participate in new friendships.
- Spend time with people to initiate and maintain friendships.
- Establish relationships and spend time with other healthy and supportive couples and families.

Purposefulness
- Create a value or purpose statement that will motivate our long-term engagement with other people.
- Survey our friends, neighbors, and community to determine where to invest our time.
- Assess the needs of our neighbors and the community in consultation with other residents, and carry out actions together to contribute to improvements.

Respect
- Ensure that community-based plans and actions are consultative and have leaders and participants from among those who will be most affected.
- Interact with people in ways that build positive mutual regard and willing cooperation.
- Contribute to and accompany others in ways that improve their lives, broaden their perspective on the community, and inspire them to demonstrate Service.

Learning Activities:

1. Identify someone or a couple with whom we want to initiate or strengthen a friendship. Consult on how to begin the process, develop a specific plan, and carry it out. Reflect on the experience afterward and consult about the next steps.

2. Plan and carry out an occasion that allows us to practice offering hospitality. Determine together what quality of experience we want our guests to have. To practice Unity, we ensure, ahead of time, that we are clear and agree on our roles and responsibilities. Assess how to manage our energy before, during, and after the activity, so we stay in balance.

3. Participate in a couples' enrichment group with like-minded couples, focusing on relationship learning and growth.

4. Invite single people who don't have a partner to dinner at our home. Encourage them to ask questions about our relationship and how we support each other in our growth.

5. Study the United Nations Sustainable Development Goals. Consult together about how they could be applied in our home. Consult with others in our neighborhood or community about which one(s) we could focus on for improvement. Create concrete plans and action steps with accountability to progress toward the chosen goal(s).

6. Meet with neighbors and consult about ways to improve the area's socio-economic conditions and/or environment. Ensure we include diverse people of all ages. Create

concrete plans and action steps with accountability to progress toward the goal.

Couple Reflection and Consultation:

Throughout this couple guide, there are invitations to practice the virtue of Reflection about your interactions and connection. This practice gives you opportunities to celebrate progress and consult to address issues.

1. What perspectives do we have about expanding our circle of unity to include others?
2. How can we begin new friendships? Establish strong and healthy friendships with other couples? Other people?
3. What can we do to sustain friendships over time?
4. How do we prepare ourselves and our home for guests? What aspects of offering hospitality make us feel happy? What stresses us instead? How can we manage that response?
5. How does hospitality expand our circle of friendships?
6. What actions do we consider particularly thoughtful or kindly helpful to a friend? A neighbor?
7. When engaging in community betterment, do we consider ourselves leaders, followers, or both?
8. Who do we know that we could invite to participate in community building or betterment with us?
9. What do we see as the needs of our community? Who could we consult with to gain a deeper understanding of them? What do we see as our role in addressing the identified needs?
10. What community groups or organizations already exist that we can collaborate with?
11. What could we carry out with specific others that would improve their lives, strengthen their ability to be

community leaders and contributors, and bring them joy? When would we act directly? Instead, when would they act while we accompany them with encouragement and consultation?

12. How else can we contribute to creating a flourishing community with our neighbors and friends?

Reflecting and Consulting on Our Vital Practices

We have been gaining new knowledge and trying new practices throughout this guide to growing our couple unity. It's useful for us to reflect, consult, and write down the most vital practices that work well for us and contribute to our maintaining a thriving relationship.

We are committed to consistently carrying out these vital practices, which are based on the Core Elements, virtues, and Unifiers. They are goals to strive for, and we also give ourselves the mercy and grace to not be perfect in achieving them. Not everything can be accomplished at once. We will have regular opportunities to:

- Use Reflection
- Consult
- Assess our progress
- Refine our vital practices
- Set new goals

Couples Share Their Experiences

Below are some additional ideas, advice, and examples from couples that we used for inspiration as we determined our most vital practices to grow and maintain our unity.

Including Virtues

We recently celebrated our 10th anniversary, so we created a list of 10 virtues that we commit to calling on for the next 10 years. The ones we chose are acceptance, compassion, creativity, discernment, grace, kindness, prayerfulness, sacrifice, trust, and dependability."

"We commit to practicing courtesy, kindness, patience, and love towards one another."

"We will use daily verbal appreciation with each other and our children in the form of Virtue Language acknowledgments."

Daily Practices

"We once received advice from an elderly couple who always seemed as if they had just fallen in love with each other. Their secret was that they never went to sleep at night upset with each other. They also turned toward each other and asked if any words or actions throughout the day had caused hurt feelings. If they had, they would apologize. If all couples practiced this, it would likely result in more successful relationships and marriages, as well as a guarantee of a good night's sleep!" [**Note:** There are times when exhaustion at night makes consulting and resolving issues at that time unwise, and waiting to address the problem is best left for the next day. Please use discernment and wisdom.]

Raising Children

"Have a family meeting or a couple's meeting and negotiate who will do what chores, ensuring a fair distribution of work. Start children on chores at a very young age by giving them a list of tasks they can complete and having them choose from it. Our boys loved this and did it every Saturday before playing or going on any outing. Our younger son, at age 3, put a happy face beside his choices, and our older son printed his name. We had a process where they took turns picking and then spent a couple of hours doing the chores. During a family consultation, they decided to do the work on Saturdays instead of every day. It worked well!"

Individual and Couple Behaviors

"We chose these commitments:

- Be friends with one another and be united in mind, body, heart, and soul.
- Treat others, especially those close to us, with love, courtesy, and integrity.
- Encourage and accompany one another's personal growth and transformation and the transformation of others.
- Regularly, lovingly, and tactfully share any hurts or annoyances we feel, using 'I feel…' terms rather than 'You do…' language. Set up a regular time to share openly and honestly.
- Demonstrate Respect for our own and each other's physical, mental, emotional, and spiritual needs, and assist each other to meet those needs as much as possible.
- Pray together daily.
- Respond to issues as quickly as possible, utilizing consultation as a tool in all matters.
- Demonstrate and accept affection and intimacy from one another on a regular basis.
- Practice Service with each other, our families, friends, and communities.
- Be playful, have fun, and incorporate humor into daily life.
- Have regular family meetings for consultation, problem-solving, and planning.
- Be patient, accepting, and nurturing, maintaining the constancy of our relationship through times of adversity and when we are not being our best selves."

Musician and vocalist Elika Mahony shared a blog posting about the significant items, in no particular order, that have contributed to the progress of her marriage to her husband, Tarry. They are:

- "Learning about the needs of one another,
- Being thoughtful,
- Paying attention to and giving priority to our relationship,
- Spending quality time together,
- Serving and praying together,
- Learning how to communicate and consult more effectively,
- Reading and studying books together on varying subjects including the subjects of love and marriage,
- Learning about each other's love language (read a book called The Five Love Languages),
- Having a weekly lunch date to check in with one another and plan (this has been especially effective),
- Having a day date occasionally (setting aside time to go for an outing)"

She added: *"Of course, there are more things on the list, but these are the ones that stood out for us."*[107]

Continuing Learning and Strengthening

"In the early part of our marriage, we discovered that reflecting on our progress every three months kept us in action. After that, we reviewed our list of vital practices as an annual part of celebrating our anniversary.

When we reflected on this year, we noticed the same item had been unfulfilled for two consecutive years. That prompted us to consider whether we were truly committed to it. When we agreed this item would still be good to have as part of our marriage, we put additional reminders and actions into place, and then we made better progress."

Creating Our Vital Practices List

1. Reflect, consult, and determine the vital practices we are committed to carrying out to grow our unity. We will include key practices from the Core Elements, Virtues, and Unifiers that are most important to us.

2. Create a visible reminder for us to keep track of our vital practices.

3. Establish a regular review interval, such as quarterly or annually, to assess our vital practices. Plan and carry out a celebration of our accomplishments. Assess this interval throughout the time ahead, as it may support us to practice Reflection daily, weekly, or monthly instead.

Reviewing Our Process

As we review what we have learned throughout this guide, we have a greater appreciation for our process of growth. We can see that we have strengthened our ability to reflect, consult, develop our virtues, and implement the Unifiers. Our connection and unity have grown, and we see that our relationship is thriving. We recognize that this is a continuous process, and we welcome it. We celebrate our progress!

Note: As you studied and practiced the Core Elements, Virtues, and Unifiers, you may have identified issues that require attention beyond the scope of this guide. We hope you will seek help from other sources, organizations, and professionals as needed. However, regardless of their issues, most people benefit from sincerely strengthening their virtues, so we hope you will do the same.

The Non-End

This book is designed for you to use repeatedly over time as your growth process continues. Referring to this material will support your growth as a couple and assist you to develop the Core Elements, virtues, and Couple Unifiers. With practice, these will become an integral part of the culture of your relationship. You will continually improve the quality of your life together.

Growing Our Unity will also accompany you in fulfilling the vision you developed in "Unifier 3: Where Are We Going?". It will accompany you as you strive to fulfill the vital practices you committed to in the last section, "Reflecting and Consulting on Our Vital Practices". Remember to put in place reminders that will prompt you to reflect, consult, and act to make progress.

You're probably noticing that your experiences as a couple are contributing to each of you strengthening your virtues. In turn, your individual growth also contributes to the quality of your couple experiences. Healthy individuals with many virtue strengths are more capable of creating couple unity.

As you grow more connected and committed as a couple, you will experience an increase in your unity. You're probably already seeing progress from your efforts so far. When you're happy as a couple, you will more consistently serve each other, your family, friends, and community, spreading happiness and unity.

Your commitment to creating a loving and fulfilling relationship will spread the powerful light of unity in the world.

Well done! Please keep on going!

Susanne M. Alexander and W. Grant Peirce IV

References

Welcome!

[1] Drs. Les and Leslie Parrott, *Relationships*, p. 11
[2] Kevin Leman, *Have a New Husband by Friday*, p. 27

Section 1: Powerfully Creating Couple Unity

[3] Raymond and Furugh Switzer, *Mindful Matrimony*, p. 259
[4] Scott M. Stanley, *Power of Commitment*, pp. 23-24
[5] "Hardwired to Connect: The New Scientific Case for Authoritative Communities", Commission on Children at Risk, 2003
[6] Summarized from Sue Johnson, *Hold Me Tight*, pp. 21-24
[7] Les and Leslie Parrott and David H. Olson, *Helping Couples*, p. 43
[8] Susan Heitler, *Power of Two*, p. 11
[9] Frank Pittman, quoted in Thomas Lickona, *Character Matters*, p. 4
[10] Blaine Fowers, *Beyond the Myth of Marital Happiness*, p. 115
[11] Harville Hendrix and Helen LaKelly Hunt, *Getting the Love You Want*, 3rd ed., p. 84
[12] John M. Gottman and Nan Silver, *Seven Principles for Making Marriage Work*, 2nd ed., p. 27

Section 2: Creating Shared Values and Vision

[13] Linda Kavelin Popov with Dan Popov, PhD, and John Kavelin, *The Family Virtues Guide*
[14] Susan Page, essay in Susanne M. Alexander, *All-in-One Marriage Prep*, pp. 284-285
[15] Stephen M. R. Covey, *The Speed of Trust*, pp. 67-68
[16] Morrie Schwartz, quoted in Mitch Albom, *Tuesdays with Morrie*, p. 149
[17] Patricia Love and Steven Stosny, *How to Improve Your Marriage Without Talking About It*, p. 100; p. 105
[18] Judith S. Wallerstein and Sandra Blakeslee, *Good Marriage*, pp. 68-69
[19] George S. Pransky, *The Relationship Handbook*, pp. 184-185
[20] W. H. Murray, *The Scottish Himalayan Expedition*, pp. 6-7

Section 3: Creating a Loving Partnership

[21] John M. Gottman and Nan Silver, *Seven Principles for Making Marriage Work*, 2nd ed., pp. 21-22; 28

[22] Shaunti Feldhahn, *The Surprising Secrets of Highly Happy Marriages*, pp. 146-147

[23] Patricia Love, *Truth About Love*, pp. 166-167

[24] Harville Hendrix and Helen LaKelly Hunt, *Getting the Love You Want*, 3rd ed., Preface, p. xx

[25] John M. Gottman and Nan Silver, *Seven Principles for Making Marriage Work*, 2nd ed., p. 54

[26] Summarized from Kathlyn Hendricks and Gay Hendricks, *Conscious Heart*, pp. 267-272

[27] Patty Howell, https://www.yourtango.com/experts/patty-howell/nurturing-yourself-widowhood-3

[28] Marshall B. Rosenberg, *Nonviolent Communication, A Language of Compassion*, 2nd ed., pp. 41-46

[29] Les and Leslie Parrott and David H. Olson, *Helping Couples*, p. 43

[30] Marital Equality: Gender and Power in Couples Therapy, http://www.marriageandfamilyresearchinstitute.com/Marital-Equality.html

[31] Kathlyn Hendricks and Gay Hendricks, *Conscious Heart,* p. 54; p. 31

[32] Mary Beth George, "What Does Trust and Commitment Look Like in a Relationship", https://www.gottman.com/blog/what-does-trust-and-commitment-look-like-in-a-relationship/

[33] Gary Chapman, T*he Five Love Languages* (1995 ed.), p. 24

[34] Summarized from Gary Chapman, *The Five Love Languages*, and quoted in Susanne M. Alexander, *Pure Gold: Encouraging Character Qualities in Marriage*, 2nd ed., p. 75

[35] Sandra Gray Bender, *Recreating Marriage with the Same Old Spouse*, pp. 11-12; p. 15

[36] Daniel C. Jordan, "Becoming Your True Self", p. 5

[37] Les and Leslie Parrott and David H. Olson, *Helping Couples*, p. 51

[38] Tara Parker-Pope, *For Better*, pp. 275-276

[39] Paul Coleman, *30 Secrets of Happily Married Couples*, p. 161

[40] Linda Kavelin Popov, *Family Virtues Guide*, p. 250

[41] Richard Carlson and Joseph Bailey, *Slowing Down to the Speed of Life*, p. 121

[42] John Gottman and Nan Silver, *Seven Principles for Making Marriage Work*, 2nd ed., p. 27

[43] Raymond and Furugh Switzer, *Mindful Matrimony*, pp. 127-128

[44] Linda Kavelin Popov, quoted in Susanne M. Alexander, *Pure Gold*, p. 52

[45] Susanne M. Alexander and Johanna Merritt Wu, *Marriage Can Be Forever—Preparation Counts!*, 4th ed., p. 110

[46] Summarized from John Gottman and Nan Silver, *Seven Principles for Making Marriage Work*, 2nd ed., Ch. 3

[47] John M. Gottman and Julie Schwartz Gottman, Level 1 Clinical Training, Gottman Method Couples Therapy, #1-4 to #1-5

[48] A.C.M.E./Better Marriages, "Creative Use of Conflict", pp. 5-7; www.bettermarriages.org, used with permission

[49] Susanne M. Alexander and Johanna Merritt Wu, *Marriage Can Be Forever—Preparation Counts!*, p. 111

[50] Les and Leslie Parrott, *When Bad Things Happen to Good Marriages*, p. 42

[51] Raymond and Furugh Switzer, *Mindful Matrimony*, pp. 128-129

[52] Shaunti Feldhahn, *Kindness Challenge*, p. 14

Section 4: Creating Connecting Experiences

[53] William J. Doherty, PhD, *Take Back Your Marriage*, p. 12

[54] John Gottman and Nan Silver, *Seven Principles for Making Marriage Work*, 2nd ed., pp. 88-89

[55] Tara Parker-Pope, *For Better*, pp. 271-272

[56] William Doherty, *Take Back Your Marriage*, pp. 130-133

[57] William Doherty, *Take Back Your Marriage*, p. 131

[58] Rob Skuka, "The Values and Rituals of Authentic Relationships: What the Relationship Enhancement Model Teaches Us About Marriage", quoted in Susanne M. Alexander, *All-in-One Marriage Prep*, pp. 282-283

[59] William Doherty, *Take Back Your Marriage*, pp. 130-133

[60] Claudia and David Arp, *10 Great Dates to Energize Your Marriage*, p. 12

[61] Jeanette C. Lauer and Robert H. Lauer, *The Play Solution*, p. 75

[62] Susan Sparks, *Laugh Your Way to Grace—Reclaiming the Spiritual Power of Humor*, pp. 9-10

[63] Stephen Post, *Why Good Things Happen to Good People*, p. 144

[64] Sharon Salzberg, *Loving-Kindness, The Revolutionary Art of Happiness*, p. 119

[65] Susan Sparks, *Laugh Your Way to Grace, Reclaiming the Spiritual Power of Humor*, p. 97

[66] Sandra Gray Bender, *Recreating Marriage with the Same Old Spouse*, p. 131

[67] "Marriage, Increase the Joy, Decrease the Misery: Service, A Key to Unlocking the Door to a Healthy and Happy Marriage", National Healthy Marriage Institute; http://healthymarriagetips.com/service.htm

[68] Willard F. Harley, Jr., *His Needs, Her Needs*, p. 19

[69] Richard Paul Evans, http://m.huffpost.com/us/entry/6958222.html

[70] Howard J. Markman, Scott M. Stanley, and Susan L. Blumberg, *Fighting for Your Marriage*, pp. 276-277

[71] Susanne M. Alexander, "Sharing Expectations and Meeting One Another's Needs"

Section 5: Forging Deeper Connection

[72] https://www.getlasting.com/marriage-advice

[73] Sue Johnson, *Hold Me Tight*, p. 186

[74] Scott Haltzman, *Secrets of Happily Married Women*, pp. 150-151

[75] Sandra Anne Taylor, *Secrets of Attraction*, p. 195

[76] Raymond and Furugh Switzer, *Mindful Matrimony*, p. 157

[77] Michele Weiner Davis, *The Sex-Starved Marriage*, pp. 11-12

[78] Barry and Emily J. McCarthy, *Getting it Right the First Time: Creating a Healthy Marriage*, pp. 78-79

[79] Syble Solomon, "With Money, What's Really Going On?" quoted in Susanne M. Alexander, *All-in-One Marriage Prep*, p. 377

[80] Natalie H. Jenkins, Scott M. Stanley, William C. Bailey, and Howard J. Markman, *You Paid How Much for That?!*, p. 17

[81] Mehri Sefidvash, *Coral and Pearls*, pp. 27-28

[82] Joan B. Hernández, *Love, Courtship, and Marriage*, p. 28

[83] Patty Howell and Ralph Jones, *World Class Marriage*, 2002 ed., p. 44

[84] Les and Leslie Parrott, *When Bad Things Happen to Good Marriages*, p. 120

[85] Les and Leslie Parrott, *When Bad Things Happen to Good Marriages*, p. 132

[86] Stephen Post, *Why Good Things Happen to Good People*, p. 114

[87] Michele Weiner-Davis, *Divorce Busting*, pp. 232-233

[88] Summarized from Gary Chapman and Jennifer Thomas, *When Sorry Isn't Enough*

[89] Les and Leslie Parrott, *When Bad Things Happen to Good Marriages*, p. 142

[90] Stephen Post, *Why Good Things Happen to Good People*, p. 104

[91] Howard J. Markman, Scott M. Stanley, Susan L. Blumberg, Natalie H. Jenkins, and Carol Whiteley, *12 Hours to a Great Marriage*, p. 207

Section 6: Expanding Beyond Us

[92] Janet A. Khan, *Prophet's Daughter*, p. 245

[93] Marriage Transformation LLC

[94] William J. Doherty, PhD, *Take Back Your Marriage*, p. 48

[95] William J. Doherty, PhD, *Take Back Your Marriage*, p. 51

[96] William J. Doherty, PhD, *Take Back Your Marriage*, p. 59

[97] Linda Kavelin Popov, *Family Virtues Guide*, pp. 29-30

[98] Monette Van Lith, *Family Matters*, p. 30

[99] Virginia Satir, *The New Peoplemaking*, Ch. 1

[100] Ron Deal, *The Smart Stepfamily*, p. 21

[101] Raymond and Furugh Switzer, *Mindful Matrimony*, p. 256

[102] Stephen R. Covey, *The 7 Habits of Highly Effective Families*, p. 72

[103] Agnes Ghaznavi, *Family Repairs and Maintenance Manual*, pp. 41-43

[104] Susan Sparks, *Laugh Your Way to Grace—Reclaiming the Spiritual Power of Humor*, p. 68

[105] Stephen Post, *Why Good Things Happen to Good People*, pp. 47; 49

[106] Paul Lample, *Creating a New Mind*, p. 112

Reflecting and Consulting on Our Vital Practices

[107] https://www.elikamahony.com; January 8, 2019

Expressing Our Gratitude

We are grateful to our families, clients, online course and workshop participants, social media connections, and more who contributed anonymously to this book. We are also grateful to the following people who generously took the time to provide input and encouragement:

Anne Bivans, Paul Blois, Glenn Booth, Raven Deerwater, Rebecca Deerwater, Fanya DeMaria, Phil Donihe, Michelle Farnsworth, Dave Grammer, Priscilla Hunt, Jane Ives, Paul Kuhn, Pat Love, Rebecca Marshall, Fiona McDonald, Ana

Morante, Richard Morris, Nisa Muhammad, Jackie Najafian, Patricia O'Connor, Deborah Peirce, Elisabeth Pereira, Guillermo Rein, Syble Solomon, Cecile Wabnitz, Johann Wong, and Johanna Merritt Wu.

Thank you to George Ronald, Publisher, for permission to quote from *Mindful Matrimony* and to Better Marriages (www.bettermarriages.org) for permission to quote from their materials.

Thank you to Linda Kavelin Popov and Dan Popov for the generous grace of encouraging Marriage Transformation to apply virtues to the relationship and marriage field.

About the Authors and Our Contact Information

Susanne M. Alexander

Susanne M. Alexander is a Relationship and Marriage Educator, book author, and publisher with Marriage Transformation®, marriagetransformation.com. She is a Certified Relationship, Pre-Marriage, and Marriage Educator and Coach through Prepare-Enrich; Certified Character Specialist; and has completed Level 1 Training in Gottman Method Couples Therapy. She is the administrator, lead facilitator, and online course developer for Transformation Learning Center, transformationlearningcenter.com/.

Susanne is passionate about facilitating consultations with individuals and couples to help them make positive choices about character, relationships, and marriage and build their knowledge and skills. Couples who make excellent choices tend to create happy, healthy relationships and marriages and prevent divorces. Susanne meets with individual and couple clients globally via the internet for character growth, relationship and marriage preparation, and couple relationship and marriage strengthening.

Susanne writes articles and books about character, relationships, and marriage. She is a member of the National Alliance for Relationship and Marriage Education (NARME).

Susanne shares: "I have had an adventurous time with relationships and marriages. My first marriage gave me a daughter, and later a son-in-law and two granddaughters. However, it was very difficult, as he had many illnesses. The marriage ended in divorce when our daughter was 18. I married again, a very happy marriage, with three young adult stepchildren. We offered marriage preparation and marriage enrichment efforts together. This second husband died from brain cancer just before our 10th wedding anniversary. Matching websites, dating experiences, and moving led me to find a third husband with two adult stepchildren, and we are in a happy marriage.

"With all these adventures and professional education, I have had many opportunities to experience, observe, and learn about the importance of finding someone with many virtue strengths to marry and then building a good marriage partnership with them. It hasn't been easy, but it's a great place to be when I have learned relationship skills and when marriage works well with love, friendship, and consultation."

Susanne is originally from Canada and now lives with her husband, Phil L. Donihe, in Tennessee, United States. They collaborate at times in working with individuals and couples. He is a coach and also certified with the Character Foundations Assessment™.

Susanne's books can be purchased in PDF format through her website, marriagetransformation.com, and paperback and ebooks are available through many online bookstores. Anyone wishing a discount on bulk purchases for group use or reselling should contact her directly.

Susanne M. Alexander
P. O. Box 249, Harrison, TN, 37341-0249, United States
+1 423.599.0153 (US Eastern time zone)
Susanne@marriagetransformation.com
https://marriagetransformation.com/
https://www.transformationlearningcenter.com/
https://www.instagram.com/marriagetransformation/
https://www.facebook.com/MarriageTransformation
https://www.linkedin.com/company/marriage-transformation
https://www.youtube.com/user/SusanneMAlexander

W. Grant Peirce IV

W. Grant Peirce IV is an Industrial and Organizational Psychologist with a passion for helping individuals and organizations succeed with integrity and purpose.

Grant serves as the Founder and CEO of Peirce Group Organizational Effectiveness Consultants. Grant is the creator of the Character Foundations Assessment™ (CFA), a validated tool designed to help individuals and organizations develop their fundamental character and make the conscious decisions necessary to achieve true and sustainable success. He is a member of the American Psychological Association, the Society for Industrial and Organizational Psychology, and the American Educational Research Association.

Grant's interest in character began with raising his daughters. He says, "They were exposed to character education at a young age. It was amazing to see how much they connected with the virtues and have used and strengthened them throughout their lives and into their young adulthood. It's still a big part of how we communicate as a family today."

After seeing the effectiveness of character education in children, Grant began to see the potential for character development in adults. "Because my profession was in organizational development, I first focused on character development for business leaders. While they found developing virtues through the CFA to be instrumental in leading their organizations, many of my clients also asked me to have their marriage partners take the CFA, so they could use the virtues to help improve their marriages."

Grant's marriage also inspires his interest in character development in couples. "Our marriage has been an adventure, starting as young graduate students in Chicago, having children, living in China for three years, moving back to Chicago, and then to Boston. We have had some real high points and some challenges, but our focus on the virtues has always kept us grounded."

Growing Our Unity is part of Grant's ongoing effort to bring character development to the entirety of people's lives. "Our personal character affects every aspect of our lives and every relationship we have. I love to see the natural joy people receive when they exhibit a character strength or when they can entice it out of others."

Grant and Deborah, his wife of 29 years, have two adult daughters, and they live in Virginia, United States.

W. Grant Peirce IV
+1 847.932.9621 (US Eastern time zone)
grantpeirce@peircegroup.com
https://www.peircegroup.com/
www.linkedin.com/in/grantpeirce

www.ingramcontent.com/pod-product-compliance
Lightning Source LLC
Chambersburg PA
CBHW062120020426

42335CB00013B/1037